Cross-Cultural Law Service

A Framework for a Lawyer's Professional Skill

Nelson P. Miller and Tracey W. Brame

Cross-cultural law service—a framework for a lawyer's professional skill.

Miller, Nelson P., and Tracey W. Brame.

Published by:

Crown Management, LLC
1527 Pineridge Drive
Grand Haven, MI 49417
USA

ISBN: 978-0-9905553-6-0

For the lawyer who knows the need to relate.

Table of Contents

Dedication v

Introduction to Cross-Cultural Skills 1

1 Intercultural: *"Could I see the other lawyer?"* 5

2 Attributive: *"They just don't get it!"* 21

3 Idiographic: *"Wasn't Einstein a white guy?"* 41

4 Historical: *"Get down on the floor!"* 55

5 Subjective: *"Another old white guy in a suit!"* 65

6 Structural: *"What did I ever do that was wrong?"* 81

7 Communicative: *"Quit fancying up his words!"* 97

8 Cognitive: *"Write down what he says!"* 117

9 Referential: *"I am blessed. And you?"* 135

10 Resourceful: *"Could someone else help me, please?"* 155

11 Relational: *"I'm not talking about you!"* 173

12 Meta-Cultural: *"Can you help me, please?"* 193

Bibliography 203

Terminology 209

Acknowledgments 213

About the Author 215

Dedication

The authors dedicate this book to Western Michigan University's Lewis Walker Institute for the Study of Race Relations. The Institute's mission is to engage in teaching, research, and service to increase understanding of race and ethnic relations, increase appreciation of the diverse peoples and cultures of the United States and other nations, and create more equitable and inclusive communities. The Institute carries out that mission through service-learning activities, poverty-reduction campaigns, community research, youth mentor programs, and many other positive community engagements. Directed since 2008 by Dr. Timothy Ready, the Institute honors the pioneering research, teaching, and service work of Emeritus Professor of Sociology Dr. Lewis Walker.

Introduction to Cross-Cultural Skills

This book's premise is simple, even though the subject is complex, satisfying, and rich. The premise is that a lawyer's effective cross-cultural service depends on the lawyer's ability to discern and adjust to a client's unique combination of attitudes, outlooks, attributes, preferences, and ambitions. This book's subsidiary premise, while not so simple, is still supremely powerful. A *framework for cross-cultural interaction* is an excellent way for a lawyer to discern quickly and adjust effectively to the client's unique combination of attitudes, outlooks, attributes, preferences, and ambitions.

The professional skills necessary to serve diverse clients effectively are much more complex than commonly assumed. A common assumption is that all that effective service to diverse clients requires is an open attitude toward the client and experience. Lawyers and others mistakenly assume that all that you need for effective cross-cultural service are good heart and attitude. Actually, though, the skills necessary for effective cross-cultural service are significantly more complex. Open attitude and willing heart are helpful but not enough. This book shows you why cross-cultural skills are complex and involve more than good attitude. You should fully appreciate the sensitivity and complexity of strong cross-cultural skills after you read the first part of this book.

Developing a clear sense of how cross-cultural interaction works can help you acquire the skills necessary for effective cross-cultural service. A sound framework can help you learn cross-cultural skills quickly and confidently. This book both explains cross-cultural skills and supplies a framework within which to practice them. Lawyers and other professionals constantly use frameworks, protocols, and heuristics that their practice helped them develop, even if only by habit, even subconsciously. This book makes evident a framework for cross-cultural service. Using this book's framework should improve your cross-cultural skills to the point that you are able to provide effective cross-cultural service.

The skills necessary for effective cross-cultural service are also keys to any effective practice, not just effective cross-cultural practice. Whether or not you ever practice cross-cultural service, you can improve your interviewing, counseling, and practice skills in any setting using this book's framework. Lawyers are most effective when they develop a meta-cultural stance, meaning a perspective beyond their own culture-bound perspective, not just in employing cross-cultural skills. Recognizing how culture influences thought, expression, and action can enable you not only to navigate and mediate your own and others' cultural influences but to choose and even create culture. This book's framework can help you vary culture and draw consciously on culture for the most effective service.

The book intersperses other authors' writings, insights, and reflections on cross-cultural experiences to give you a sense of the breadth, depth, and richness of the literature touching on cross-cultural service. Use these additional readings to enjoy and continue your exploration of this important and unendingly fascinating subject. The book also illustrates many of its concepts using law-practice vignettes. It does so to help you see how practical these concepts are in practice. While the book has a certain amount of theory behind it, the authors intend it to be practical and clinical, not theoretical. The book also includes a few vignettes drawn from personal experiences. Professional knowledge, skill, and identity can and often should draw from personal experience. Personal experience informs a lawyer's own culture including the lawyer's attitude, outlook, attributes, preferences, and ambitions. You must first discover who you are in order to appreciate the identity of others. The personal vignettes are to show you how you can connect personal experience to professional identity.

Finally, each of the book's chapters concludes with a series of questions meant to encourage you to reflect on the concepts, develop the insights, and practice the skills that the chapter addresses. Lawyers do not practice in a personal vacuum. We have our own lives and experiences. Write, understand, and share your own story to better hear, understand, and tell the story of others.

Chapter 1

Intercultural

"Could I see the *other* lawyer?"

An Example of Ineffective Service

The lawyer had been seeing pro bono clients one or two afternoons a week for a few years at a church in a rough neighborhood of an economically depressed Midwestern rust-belt city. The church had a vibrant African-American congregation with a rich spiritual and social ministry to the poor and disadvantaged. The lawyer enjoyed the work, even though making time for it out of a busy litigation practice created a certain amount of stress. The pastor, a saint, appreciated the relief that the free law services afforded him from dealing with issues that were legal rather than spiritual.

A retired lawyer heard of the first lawyer's work. Intrigued, the retired lawyer offered to share the work with the lawyer. They started to alternate weeks. It lasted just two weeks. Clients insisted, even if politely, on seeing the *other* lawyer—the lawyer who had long been providing the pro bono service. The clients perceived that the retired lawyer lacked some skill that evidently the first lawyer possessed. Even though the service was free, clients refused to see the retired lawyer. For his part, the retired lawyer complained quietly to the first lawyer about the clients, that they just did not seem to want to *listen* to him.

Searching for an Explanation

The retired lawyer's failure disappointed and puzzled the first lawyer. The retired lawyer did not lack compassion. The retired lawyer and his wife were the dearest of souls. It had been the retired lawyer's idea that he should help with the pro bono service. The retired lawyer looked and acted like a kind uncle, a sober, responsible, and trustworthy soul. The retired lawyer was also punctual, prepared, and readily available. He had all the time in the world. He had arrived early for the work, taken as much time as anyone wished, and stayed late. The retired lawyer was not careless or unskilled. He had been primarily a transactional lawyer and estate planner, serving a middle-class and even well-to-do clientele. He was thoughtful, knowledgeable, cautious, and highly skilled.

By contrast, the first lawyer was not retired and did not really have the time out of a busy litigation practice, although the lawyer took the time anyway. The first lawyer tended to keep the several compressed appointments short, sweet, and to the point. The first lawyer needed to get back to the office quickly to try to complete what he could of the pro bono work without falling behind on the constant cavalcade of tasks from the lawyer's paying work. While the lawyer judged himself to be competent and adequately skilled to help the pro bono clients, he still felt that if he needed free legal help of the kind that he had been providing, then he would have chosen the retired lawyer rather than himself.

Yet the first lawyer knew the retired lawyer well enough to sense, just barely, what the retired lawyer may have lacked. The first lawyer could not exactly put his finger on it, could not articulate specifically the retired lawyer's missing skills. Nor could the first lawyer describe what he apparently possessed that the retired lawyer lacked. The lawyer needed to know why the retired lawyer's service had not worked. If the first lawyer had some skill that the retired lawyer did not, then that skill was merely an underdeveloped, nascent, and hidden skill. The first lawyer needed to know the skill if he had any hope of improving on it and of sharing it with other lawyers.

"Judicial, prosecutorial, and defense agencies across the country face significant challenges as they strive to effectively serve their increasingly diverse communities. One of the keys to successfully navigating these challenges is cultural competence—the ability to interact effectively with people of different cultures. Psychological research tells us, however, that implicit social bias, independent from one's explicit values and beliefs about equity and fairness, is hard-wired into the human experience in a way that hinders one's ability to interact with others in a culturally competent manner, even in the absence of explicit bias.

"The reality of implicit bias has significant implications for participants in the criminal justice system. Growing evidence suggests that subconscious prejudices and implicit bias affect an astonishing range of human interaction. In the criminal justice system, implicit bias can affect important issues, such as policing patterns and practices, decisions to hire and promote employees within criminal justice agencies, and jury deliberations and sentencing decisions in the courtroom.

"The good news is that cultural competence can be cultivated to help navigate this complex terrain. Increasing cultural competency skills holds the promise of providing leaders and managers of prosecution, defense, and court agencies with the information, training, and resources they need to create culturally competent work environments. Such environments allow leaders and managers to effectively address personnel, communication, and management issues related to race and culture, and to recruit, retain, and promote a diverse work force. Increasing cultural competency skills has the added benefit of introducing a common language for addressing the racial disparities inherent in the American criminal justice system and for engaging in the challenging discussion that could lead to more effective solutions. Ultimately, increasing cultural competency skills can help to improve community perceptions of and confidence in the criminal justice system by helping judges, prosecutors, and defenders understand how these perceptions arise. Doing so will also teach those in the justice system how to make decisions that are culturally sensitive and judicially appropriate and that build respect for the rule of law." American Bar Association, *Building Community Trust: Improving Cross-cultural Communication in the Criminal Justice System* 1-2 (June 2010).

Practicing the Skills

The first lawyer's disappointment, frustration, and curiosity over the retired lawyer's inability to serve diverse clients inspired and spurred the academic and clinical research that led to this book. For the next several years, the lawyer provided pro bono service at various community sites, first while practicing law and later as a law professor's service component. The lawyer made a point of varying the service sites. Each site served a different client population. Each client population exhibited some of the same but then again also different problems, issues, needs, and preferences. Each population also brought unique individuals.

The lawyer provided pro bono service once per week or once per month at three different African-American churches in three different cities. One congregation was in a middle socioeconomic class, one in a lower socioeconomic class, and one in the lowest socioeconomic class. The lawyer also provided weekly pro bono service at a Hispanic-American cultural center and periodic service at a Hispanic-American chamber of commerce. Most of that work was through translators. Nearly all of it was for immigrants, many of them undocumented.

The lawyer also provided pro bono service at a soup kitchen every week and at a homeless mission and residential substance-abuse treatment center once per month, each for several years. The soup kitchen and homeless mission served immigrants, recently released prisoners, the mentally disabled, and victims of domestic violence, among others. The lawyer also provided periodic on-base pro bono service to military service-members and once-per-year service to disabled veterans. The lawyer also provided periodic patron service at a courthouse self-help center and helped to govern the center through board and officer service.

In all, the lawyer saw over 2,500 pro bono clients over a period of about a decade, working out to about five pro bono consultations a week. The lawyer also litigated civil-rights cases retaining and involving diversity experts. The lawyer also served for many years on his state bar's diversity committee. There, he heard, read about, and discussed the laudable efforts of others to ensure that the profession is diverse and supports the diversity skills of lawyers.

The Value of Observation

Pro bono work gave the lawyer the opportunity not only to practice the skills necessary to serve diverse clients but also to observe other lawyers, law students, and service professionals practice those skills. Law students accompanied the lawyer on many of those service visits. Some of the lawyers, law students, and other professionals were ineffective, others effective, and a few masterful in interacting with diverse clients. The wide range from ineffectiveness to effectiveness that the lawyer observed confirmed for him that cross-cultural service involved not merely compassion but also definite if subtle skills.

The law student whose mastery the lawyer recalled most vividly was a 50-year-old former pastor and performing musician. The student was so good at connecting with every client that on the couple of pro bono service visits that they attended together, the lawyer learned to simply sit back, watch, and quietly supply any necessary legal analysis and information that the still-new law student could not supply. Despite that the lawyer exhibited the law knowledge that the student in certain instances clearly lacked, the student's confident, reassuring, respectful, and supportive manner was so powerful that clients listened to the student, not the lawyer. The student also displayed subtly different skills with different clients.

The observations proved that an effective lawyer is not one who is simply free of cultural associations implicating some form of bias or prejudice. Effective service to diverse clients requires more than simply refraining from thinking or saying the wrong thing in a manner that exhibits bias. Being free of all bias is likely impossible, especially without a framework through which to recognize bias. Even if it were possible never to harbor any negative associations based on class membership, then doing so would not be sufficient for effective professional service. Legal service involves appropriate action more so than merely a guilt-free state of mind.

The premise that any competent lawyer can serve any client underestimates the range of skills that masterful lawyers employ.

Effective lawyers do not merely analyze in the formal manner associated with law school instruction. Indeed, culturally aware lawyers avoid the trap of the mono-cultural language and logic skills, and formal judgments, emphasized early in law school. Sensitive lawyers instead employ a range of affirmative affective skills serve, relate to, communicate with, and gain the confidence and trust of diverse clients. Culturally sensitive lawyers employ skills that bridge cultures. They develop and use emotional, social, and affective adaptations that carry them above the limitations of discrete and insular culture.

The problem with effective service is *not* with the diverse client's culture. The obstacle to effective professional service is instead often the lawyer's *professional* culture. Effective lawyers recognize and adapt to the client's culture and context. They preserve and amplify rather than ignore or destroy the social and moral content of their clients' experiences. Lawyers who master effective interaction with diverse clients see professional service not merely as arms-length transactions but as interdependent relationships. Far from being inflexible, fixed, or rigid with clients, effective lawyers possess and exercise a richly complex range of alternative responses. Effective lawyers are able to converse with, relate to, appreciate, and serve diverse clients not in *spite of* cultural differences but rather *drawing on* powerful cultural context.

"During my term as President of the American Bar Association, I chose to highlight one of the most pressing issues in the justice system: the alarming lack of racial and ethnic minority representation in the legal profession. The data are compelling. Presently, our profession is more than 90 percent white, and enrollment in our law schools is about 80 percent white. But 30 percent of our society are people of color, and in the next few decades it will be 50 percent. These trends put at risk our profession's historic role as the connecting link between our society and the rule of law. One of our goals this year was to establish a foundation for future work by building on successful existing programs that have advanced the cause of diversity in the profession." William G. Paul, President, American Bar Association, July 2000.

Academic Research

To balance with academic perspective the clinical experience of serving diverse populations, the lawyer also researched, wrote, presented, and collaborated in writing and presenting on the subject of diversity skills and training. The lawyer wrote articles for law reviews and bar journals, and book chapters. The lawyer presented at a law review symposium and conducted workshops with and for administrators, faculty, and students. The lawyer also headed a law school's participation in a diversity compact among several local colleges and universities. That leadership allowed the lawyer to make, attend, and arrange for presentations on the subject, and to meet in groups and privately with diversity experts to learn about cross-cultural skills and assess the lawyer's work and his campus's work.

This effort, and the articulate, insightful, and committed people involved in it, helped the lawyer develop the perspective and locate, identify, and promote the tools that this book describes. Acknowledgments at the end of the book list six co-authored book chapters and articles from which the authors drew portions of this book. The bibliography lists an additional 60 writings informing and contributing to the author's perspective. Clinical experience and academic research work hand in hand to improve professional reflection and development.

The Need for Diversity Skills

Whatever the diversity skills are, American lawyers have always had the need for them. Almost no matter the field, law practice expects lawyers to serve unlike others. Lawyers in so many different fields must relate effectively to diverse populations. Think of immigration lawyers, maritime lawyers, and lawyers who deal with customs, tariffs, treaties, and trade. They constantly work across international boundaries. Yet think also of prosecutors and defenders, dealing with crimes involving victims, suspects, and perpetrators from all demographics. Think also of municipal lawyers dealing with the interests of all members of a community, whether rich or poor, old or young, advantaged or disadvantaged, transient or resident.

11

Skills to serve diverse clients are critical in a nation that properly prides itself not only on its multiculturalism and openness but even on its discrete populations and regionalism. Think of family lawyers, dealing with divorce, custody and paternity disputes, support needs, and abuse and neglect, each of which knows no socioeconomic or ethnic boundaries. Think also of personal-injury attorneys, workers-compensation counsel, and Social Security lawyers dealing with injury, disability, and disease from which no individual has immunity. Think also of employment lawyers, civil-rights lawyers, public-interest lawyers, and insurance-defense counsel, dealing with all segments of society having different skills, experiences, issues, and needs. Even estate planners, tax lawyers, transactional lawyers, business litigators, and real-estate lawyers may serve exceedingly diverse client populations.

> "Allow me to say, in conclusion, notwithstanding the dark picture I have this day presented of the state of the nation, I do not despair of this country. There are forces in operation, which must inevitably work the downfall of slavery. 'The arm of the Lord is not shortened,' and the doom of slavery is certain. I, therefore, leave off where I began, with hope. While drawing encouragement from the Declaration of Independence, the great principles it contains, and the genius of American Institutions, my spirit is also cheered by the obvious tendencies of the age. Nations do not now stand in the same relation to each other that they did ages ago. No nation can now shut itself up from the surrounding world." Frederick Douglass, *Oration Delivered in Corinthian Hall, Rochester* (1852), in JONATHAN BEAN, ED., RACE AND LIBERTY IN AMERICA: THE ESSENTIAL READER 40-41 (Univ. of Kentucky Press 2009).

The Need Increases

Lawyers have always needed and often exercised the skills to bridge gaps in understanding, language, context, and experience. America's diversity is certainly not new. Nantucket was already highly diverse when Melville wrote in *Moby Dick* of its cosmopolitan mid-19th-century wharf, from which the fictional Captain Ahab drew his crew of Ishmael, Elijah, the Polynesian Queequeg, Parsee Fedallah, and Quaker Starbuck. Imagine a lawyer advising the Pequod's crew on immigration, employment, maritime, personal-injury, and wrongful-death law. Harper Lee in the mid-20th-century novel *To Kill a Mockingbird* set lawyer Atticus Finch within a southern society presenting a very different but equally challenging kind of diversity. Real lawyers from Lincoln and Darrow to Thurgood Marshall and Johnnie Cochran have needed and used cross-cultural skills.

The need for lawyers to have the skills to serve diverse populations may nonetheless be increasing with increasing globalization of economies and businesses, and increasing migration of labor. The year 2000 census identified the Hispanic population as 13% of United States population, African Americans at 12%, and Asian Americans at 4%, with significant numbers of Native Americans, Alaska Natives, Pacific Islanders, and other populations. The year 2010 census showed these populations increasing to 16% Hispanic, 13% African American, and 5% Asian Americans. Projections have these populations continuing to grow in numbers and percentages significantly. The challenge, though, is not just to meet global changes. The challenge is also to serve the significant percentage of those whom lawyers presently underserve in their civil legal needs. For lawyers to lack the skills to serve diverse populations is to contribute to the existing underrepresentation of these populations. For lawyers to acquire those skills is to open the door to justice and the economic and social prosperity that come with it.

> "The ABA Commission on Racial and Ethnic Diversity in the Profession is a diverse group of committed lawyers serving, through its work and programs, as the catalyst for creating leadership and economic opportunities for racially and ethnically diverse lawyers within the and the legal profession. We provide a voice to surface and tackle issues of discrimination, racism and bigotry, and to inspire the profession to value differences, to be sensitive to prejudice, and to reflect the society we serve." Reginald M. Turner, Jr., Chair, ABA Commission on Racial and Ethnic Diversity.

Jargon Warning

This book avoids some of the socio-cultural jargon employed to varying degrees within diversity studies. See the bibliography at the end of this book for academic and scholarly literature using that jargon to good effect. This book is practical, not academic. Yet naming things can help one understand and control them. Learning just a little jargon can help, even if just long enough to learn new skills. Once you learn the skill, forget the jargon. Simply understand for now some terms used to identify and examine group and individual behavior. See also the terminology list at the back of the book.

Understanding Culture

Culture is the shared set of norms, understandings, or beliefs guiding behavior within populations and across generations. Culture has powerful influences, both positive and negative. Culture influences who we are and what we remain or become.

A large part of a lawyer's professional success has to do with learning and employing the professional culture of law practice. Law practice has its own norms, customs, habits, and practices. It has its own ways. To mention briefly subjects that this book addresses in depth later, professional culture has its own *language register*, *cognitive preferences*, *reference points*, *resources*, and *relationships*. Law schools are extremely effective at introducing law students to the profession's culture. Law students make profound changes in their language, dress, thought patterns, commitments, and beliefs during law school. What law schools do not teach, law firms do. The first few years of law practice form lawyer identity just as effectively as law school does, or more so. Law practice augments, sharpens, and confirms a new lawyer's professional culture.

When dealing with one another and with service providers like property managers, bankers, financial advisors, accountants, expert witnesses, and other administrative professionals, lawyers operate within professional cultures similar to their own professional culture. Professions have their own subcultures, but culture across administrative professions is relatively uniform. Professionals work well together in large part because of the uniformity or similarity of their norms, customs, habits, practices, and assumptions.

Take as an example the helpful retired lawyer whose lack of cross-cultural skill introduced this chapter. The professional culture into which law school trained that lawyer and the law practice that steeped him is distinct from non-professional culture. The retired lawyer walked, talked, thought, and related like other lawyers generally relate to one another and to other administrative professionals. The retired lawyer's knowledge of law and of a lawyer's ways was what gave the first lawyer such confidence in his offer to help with pro bono services.

"A broad definition of culture (and its multiplicity of potential sources) is important for several reasons. It alerts students and lawyers to a fuller range of background influences that can shape people and interactions. It thus encourages us to broaden our horizons and to attend to multiple layers of potential meaning. It also highlights that a lawyer cannot become complacent simply because she shares one or more cultural identities with her client. ... [O]thers have addressed the risks that such complacency can lead lawyers to presume, rather than to explore, clients' values and preferences, and to ignore dynamics—such as other dimensions of cultural difference—that lead clients to still perceive the lawyer as an outsider. A broad definition of culture, in short, makes cross-cultural competency relevant for all lawyers." Ascanio Piomelli, *Cross-Cultural Lawyering by the Book: The Latest Clinical Texts and a Sketch of a Future Agenda*, 4 HASTINGS RACE & POVERTY L.J. 131, 151 (2006) (footnotes omitted).

Examining Culture

To ignore culture is to some degree to remain a prisoner bound by it. To be culture-bound is to be unaware of the limiting forms of one's own culture. Culture can aid or hinder a lawyer's service, depending on the practices that its beliefs discourage or promote. A lawyer's knowledge of culture tends to neutralize and place within the lawyer's control the culture's effect on the lawyer's ability to provide cross-cultural service. Lawyers become more effective in cross-cultural service when they can identify and alter their own culturally bound practices. The more-sensitive and therefore more-effective practices are ones that you choose, not ones that the profession's culture or culture of a prior generation impose on you while you remain unaware of that culture's effect and limitation.

15

The way that most lawyers generally think, relate, and speak is not universal. Professional culture limits and binds any lawyer who thinks that the lawyer's way is the universal way. It is not. Individuals who do not have a lawyer's training do not think, speak, and relate like a lawyer, and nor should they. While lawyers have highly valuable skills of which lawyer culture is an important part, the world would be no better if we were all lawyers or all bound by lawyer culture. An underlying premise of this book is that examining culture long enough to recognize its presence, proclivities, and limitations frees one from its limiting effects, a premise treated in much greater depth later.

Take as an example the helpful retired lawyer who failed to recognize that he was operating within a peculiar professional culture. That failure was his professional undoing in interacting with the first lawyer's pro bono clients. When the first lawyer tried gently to find out why clients did not want to see the retired lawyer, the clients gave answers like "he didn't seem to understand," "he didn't get it," and "we couldn't relate." The clients had no complaints about the retired lawyer's knowledge, dress, or comportment. Indeed, the retired lawyer looked, spoke, and acted every part a lawyer, which was ultimately his problem. The retired lawyer did not recognize how powerfully professional culture had shaped and constrained his work, frustrating the pro bono clients who quickly declined his service.

Intercultural Skills

Intercultural means operating across cultures. While lawyers tend to work with other lawyers and professionals within relatively uniform professional culture, by contrast many of the services that lawyers provide to clients are intercultural services. Clients do not generally share lawyer culture, unless of course the clients are lawyers, legal assistants, or other administrative professionals.

Lawyers who are effective at counseling clients, and especially diverse clients, recognize that they subtly change behaviors when they go from interacting with other lawyers and administrative professionals to counseling clients. A lawyer's behavioral changes are not simply in terminology, in the words that the lawyer chooses. The changes may also be in emotion, demeanor, voice, cognitive conventions, worldview, resource assumptions, and relationship preferences. Again, you will read much more about those changes later. Indeed, this book's purpose is to help you recognize what those changes are and organize them into a useful framework, so that you can make those changes most effectively for the greatest number and widest variety of clients.

Interaction across cultures can promote your knowledge of culture. It can also help you understand how powerfully culture works. Study of that interaction can accelerate how you acquire intercultural skills. Lawyers, like other administrative professionals, and the college-educated generally, can benefit from training in inter-cultural practices. The Clinical Legal Education Association's *Best Practices* report emphasizes that lawyers should be sensitive and effective when serving diverse clients. The goal of intercultural competence is to enable you to serve across cultures in a respectful and engaged manner that builds and preserves the client's trust necessary for your professional service to be effective. Intercultural skills are critical to effective service when you work across cultures.

Objectives

This book's goal is that readers will acquire the intercultural awareness and exercise the intercultural skills necessary to serve clients having diverse communication forms, cognitive practices, cultural references, resource capabilities, and relationship needs. If you read this book closely, reflecting with effort and insight on the questions that it poses, then you should be able to:

- identify your own communication register, identify variety in client communication registers, distinguish your communication register from those of specific clients in specific situations, and adjust your communication register accordingly for effective advice and counsel to diverse clients;

- identify your own cognitive practices, identify variety in client cognitive practices, distinguish your cognitive practices from those of specific clients in specific situations, and adjust your cognitive practices accordingly for effective advice and counsel to diverse clients;

- identify your own cultural references, identify variety in client cultural references, distinguish your cultural references from specific clients in specific situations, and adjust your cultural references accordingly for effective advice and counsel to diverse clients;

- identify your own resource advantages, identify variety in client resources, distinguish your resource advantages from those of specific clients in specific situations, and adjust your resource planning accordingly for effective advice and counsel to diverse clients; and

- identify your own relationship preferences, identify variety in client relationship preferences, distinguish your relationship preferences from specific clients in specific situations, and adjust your relationship practices accordingly for effective advice and counsel to diverse clients.

Pursuing these objectives should help you accomplish the overall goal, which again is to work more frequently, productively, and effectively in a variety of settings with diverse clients, in a respectful manner conducive to the benefit of clients and the community as a whole. You might also influence others to do the same.

Reflections

Consider the following reflections on inter-cultural skills. Begin a journal of your reflections. Find someone who shares your professional interests with whom to discuss these questions:

1. On a scale from 1 to 10, how do you rate your inter-cultural skills serving diverse clients as a lawyer? What criteria would you articulate to measure intercultural skills?

2. Assuming that a large corporate client interviewed you for a representation that required strong intercultural skills, what evidence would you offer of your intercultural skills serving diverse clients as a lawyer? What experiences do you have on

which you might be able to draw to illustrate your intercultural skills?

3. Identify a lawyer (or if you cannot think of a lawyer then another professional or person) whom you regard as having strong intercultural skills. What skills distinguish that person's performance? What education, training, or experience does that person have that might have given that person an advantage in acquiring intercultural skills? What difference do those skills make for the person's ability to relate well to diverse individuals? How do those skills enrich the person professionally, financially, socially, and otherwise?

4. What cross-cultural skills (communication, cultural reference, personal relationship, time or resource sharing, etc.) or attitudes (patience, perseverance, empathy, curiosity, flexibility, etc.) are your strengths? How did you develop those strengths? How could you develop them further? Where could you best exhibit them in professional representation and service?

5. Where are your cross-cultural weaknesses (communication, cultural reference, personal relationship, time or resource sharing, patience, perseverance, empathy, curiosity, flexibility, etc.)? Why are you weak in those areas? How might you remediate those weaknesses?

6. What professional representation or experience (service in a second language, translated service, cross-ethnic service, service to a religious community, international-client service, overseas legal work, mission work, etc.) would you most like to have in the future that would draw or depend on your strong intercultural skills? Why attracts you to that representation or experience?

Chapter 2

Attributive

"They just don't get it!"

Group-Based Attribution

When the two lawyers met some months later, the subject of the retired lawyer's failed effort to help the first lawyer out with cross-cultural pro bono services came up once again. The first lawyer was happy to ignore the subject in favor of the good relationship that the two lawyers shared. So, the retired lawyer had not been able to help the clients. In the larger scheme of things, what did that failure really matter? Yet the retired lawyer could not leave the subject alone. Unable or unwilling to attribute his failure to his own knowledge or skills, he turned instead to the character and capacities of the clients. Referring alternately to the client population's ethnicity and to that ethnicity's supposed culture, the retired lawyer decried a general lack of commitment and skill, and suggested a laziness leading, the retired lawyer inferred, to their low income levels.

"That must explain it," the retired lawyer concluded, adding, "What a waste of time. Those people just don't get it!"

As the retired lawyer spoke, the first lawyer cringed, not even trying to hide the reaction. The retired lawyer's assertions seemed to the first lawyer to have been non-sequiturs. Of course the clients had low incomes. They were seeing a lawyer for free legal service in a busy church office. Members of the same population who had higher income levels would not have been seeking free legal service. Indeed, they would have been living in different neighborhoods with more-expensive housing, easy access to transportation, more public and private amenities, and ready access to legal services. Simply because the confused affairs of the few particular clients whom the retired lawyer had seen in his couple of service attempts may have shown lack of skill, sophistication, and attention did not mean that a culture or ethnicity shared those particulars.

Maybe some minority clients and perhaps within certain geographic areas even a disproportionate number of them would have given insufficient attention to their affairs. Yet what would those observations have necessarily to do with the attention that other minority clients in that area and other areas would have given to their affairs. The first lawyer knew that many members of that community were scrupulous in every financial, legal, and other administrative matter, whether they had high or low levels of skill. The retired lawyer nonetheless justified his inability to help the few clients he had seen to cultural and ethnic characteristics.

> "I conceive ... that there is no division of races. God Almighty made but one race. I adopt the theory that in time the varieties of races will be blended into one. Let us look back when the black and the white people were distinct in this country. In two hundred and fifty years there has brown up a million of intermediate. And this will continue. You may say that Frederick Douglass considers himself a member of the one race which exists." Frederick Douglass, *Mr. Douglass Interview* (Washington Post, Jan. 26, 1884), in JONATHAN BEAN, ED., RACE AND LIBERTY IN AMERICA: THE ESSENTIAL READER 98 (Univ. of Kentucky Press 2009).

The Problem of Over-Inclusiveness

When the retired lawyer attributed poor administrative skills to a culture and ethnicity, the lawyer was extending his limited observations of a very few clients to attribute similar limitations to a vast group with whom the lawyer had little or no direct familiarity. The retired lawyer had not served a substantial minority population, locally or elsewhere. The retired lawyer nonetheless declined further service attempts based on attributions he was ready to make generally.

We each have experiences. The retired lawyer asserted experiences with minority clients. Yet the problem of over-inclusiveness arises when we extend those experiences to predict attributes, qualifications, and behaviors of others beyond the observed individuals. The challenge in overcoming over-inclusiveness is to be sure that one does not attribute characteristics to persons whom one has *not* observed simply because they share *other* characteristics, such as membership in an ethnic group, that one *has* observed. Lawyers should not assume that a client has certain attributes simply because the client shares other characteristics, like similar ethnicity, ancestry, origin, hairstyle, dress, lifestyle, income level, or neighborhood residence, with clients or other persons with whom the lawyer has experience.

> "The plaintiff [Dred Scott] was a negro slave, belonging to Dr. Emerson, who was a surgeon in the army of the United States. In the year 1834, he took the plaintiff from the State of Missouri to the military post at Rock Island, in the State of Illinois....
>
> "In the year 1836, the plaintiff and [another slave] Harriet intermarried, at Fort Snelling, with the consent of Dr. Emerson, who then claimed to be their master and owner. Eliza and Lizzie ... are the fruit of that marriage. ...
>
> "In the year 1838, said Dr. Emerson removed the plaintiff and said Harriet, and their said daughter Eliza, from said Fort Snelling to the State of Missouri, where they have ever since resided.
>
> "Before the commencement of this suit, said Dr. Emerson sold and conveyed the plaintiff, and Harriet, Eliza, and Lizzie, to the defendant, as slaves, and the defendant has ever since claimed to hold them, and each of them, as slaves.
>
> "... [T]wo questions arise: 1. Was [Dred Scott], together with his family, free in Missouri ...? And 2. If they were not, is Scott himself free by reason of his removal to Rock Island, in the State of Illinois, as stated in the above admissions? ...
>
> "[I]t is the judgment of this court, that ... [Dred Scott] is not a citizen of Missouri, in the sense in which that word is used in the Constitution; and that the Circuit Court of the United States, for that reason, had no jurisdiction in the case, and could give no judgment in it. ..." Dred Scott v. Sandford, 60 U.S. 393, 431-432, 454 (1856).

Generalizing Over-Inclusive Attributions

Anyone can make over-inclusive attributions. Group members sometimes even make those attributions against members of their own groups. People also generalize over-inclusive attributions beyond any specific experience that they have with a member of the group. Consider another example.

The African-American pastor was thanking the Caucasian-American lawyer for giving pro bono legal service to his African-American congregants. The lawyer said that he looked forward to the day when the congregation had lawyers within their own community to whom they could turn for legal services.

"Oh, don't worry about that," the pastor rejoined, adding, "They'll think they're not getting the best."

The lawyer thought he had misunderstood the pastor. He asked what the pastor meant.

"Lawyers, doctors—it's the same with any professional," the pastor explained. "If you send a minority lawyer in here, my people will think that they are not getting the best help that they need for their problems."

Years later, the congregation had competent African-American lawyers among its members to whom the members gladly turned. The challenge of over-inclusive attribution is to recognize and reject attributions that are inappropriately class based, whether or not the attribution has a basis in an initial experience with a single member of the class. Simply because one is a member of the class does not mean that one has greater rationale to generalize attributes to the class.

The Problem of Inaccurate Attribution

Another odd part about the retired lawyer's attributions (in addition to the openness with which the lawyer had shared his view and that he had extended his view beyond its observed factual basis) was that when the first lawyer investigated whom the retired lawyer had tried to serve, indeed followed up with those clients to ensure that they received appropriate help, the first lawyer discovered that the clients' matters did not indicate any gross lack of skill, attention, or commitment. To the first lawyer, their problems seemed like any other client's problems, just beyond the client's ability to resolve, but yet a problem that the client was plenty willing to address with due attention. Not only were the retired lawyer's assertions over-inclusive as to the culture and ethnicity, but their bases were also factually inaccurate.

The retired lawyer could have addressed these clients' problems. The clients wanted and needed them addressed and were more than willing to do as the retired lawyer could have advised. Yet the retired lawyer's interpretation and assertions were that the clients were indifferent to their own self-made problems. Sometimes, we see patterns where they do not exist. The human mind is so powerful in its effort to construct meaning that we sometimes construct false premises.

We should recognize some of the assumptions that might have caused the retired lawyer to construct his inaccurate premise. He had a deep concern to improve the lives of these clients. Given that outlook, and the frustration he developed in trying to accomplish his professional objective, the retired lawyer would have found it easy to assume obstacles to and failures in his clients' problem-solving skills.

The challenge in overcoming inaccurate attribution is to be sure that one does not attribute characteristics to a person without investigating and obtaining reliable data on that person. Moreover, one must not attribute characteristics to a member of a group based on tendencies that may exist in that group, without first confirming that the member actually has those tendencies. Lawyers should not make assumptions about clients and other persons without reliable data supporting those assumptions. A lawyer's inferences should be data-based and accurate.

"Culture influences the way people express themselves, including everything from tone of voice, being 'polite' or 'argumentative,' using lots of gestures, and even saying yes when the real answer is no. Understanding the norms of the culture a person comes from can help communication enormously...." Lois J. Zachary, The Mentor's Guide: Facilitating Effective Learning Relationships 42-43 (Jossey Bass 2d ed. 2012).

The Problem of Under-Inclusiveness

Another odd part about the retired lawyer's observations was that higher-income, majority-ethnicity clients in the retired lawyer's usual practice population likely had approximately the same incidence of legal, financial, and other administrative issues as these low-income minority clients did. The first lawyer served that same higher-income, majority-ethnicity client population as the retired lawyer had. The first lawyer knew the wide variation in legal, financial, and administrative skills, and emotional capacity and personal commitment, within that majority-ethnicity population. So the retired lawyer could just as easily have attributed lack of commitment to his majority-ethnicity clients as he did to these low-income minority pro bono clients, in any particular instance. In that respect, the retired lawyer's conclusion about minority clients lacking commitment or being lazy was *under*-inclusive as to majority-ethnicity clients who across the full population had equivalent characteristics.

Under-inclusion is to attribute characteristics solely to a person or subgroup when those same characteristics appear in the same distribution across the whole group of which the person is a member or subgroup is a part. The challenge in overcoming under-inclusiveness is to ensure that one does not attribute characteristics solely to a person or group when others outside of that person or group have the same characteristics. Anytime that a lawyer begins to think that all members of a certain population share certain habits or attributes, then the lawyer should look for individuals among broader populations for the same habits and attributes. One will readily find them, highlighting the under-inclusiveness problem.

Jargon Warning

Here it is again, the jargon. Follow it just long enough to get the gist of the involved skills. Then forget the jargon while remembering the skills. You should simply understand from precise and distinct terminology the fundamental problem that negative group-based attribution presents.

Pathological Attribution

Pathic is a suffix or combining form meaning to suffer a recognized illness, distortion, or disease, such as in *pathology* meaning the study of disease or *osteopathic* meaning to correct a diseased condition by manipulation of bones or other body parts. The adjective *pathological* means so far out of the healthy normal as to be grossly distorted or diseased in a way that affects one's ability to live or perform well socially. A behavior becomes *pathological* when it harms the one who exhibits it and others around that person.

More to the point, pathological *attribution* is to attribute negative characteristics to a person who does not have those characteristics, in a way that undermines the person and relationship. One form of pathological attribution would be to attribute a negative characteristic to a person because the person bears some similarity in other *neutral* characteristics to a person who or group that demonstrates a prevalence of that negative characteristic. So, for instance, one might find a higher incidence of suicide, depression, or even violent behavior within combat veterans. Yet to attribute any of those characteristics to a specific veteran could be pathological, undermining and harming the professional making the attribution, the veteran, and the professional relationship.

"... Plessy ... was assigned by officers of the company to the coach used for the race to which he belonged, but he insisted upon going into a coach used by the race to which he did not belong. ...

"[Plessy claimed that he] was seven-eighths Caucasian and one-eighth African blood; that the mixture of colored blood was not discernible in him; and that he was entitled to every right, privilege, and immunity secured to citizens of the United States of the white race; and that, upon such theory, he took possession of a vacant seat in a coach where passengers of the white race were accommodated, and was ordered by the conductor to vacate said coach, and take a seat in another, assigned to persons of the colored race, and, having refused to comply with such demand, he was forcibly ejected, with the aid of a

---

police officer, and imprisoned in the parish jail to answer a charge of having violated the above act.

"The constitutionality of this act is attacked upon the ground that it conflicts both with the thirteenth amendment of the constitution, abolishing slavery, and the fourteenth amendment, which prohibits certain restrictive legislation on the part of the states. ...

"[T]he question of the proportion of colored blood necessary to constitute a colored person, as distinguished from a white person, is ... to be determined under the laws of each state....

"The judgment of the court below is therefore affirmed."   Plessy v. Ferguson, 163 U.S. 537, 549, 552 (1896).

The Problem of Pathological Attribution

Attribution by group characteristics can readily lead to inappropriately pathological conceptualizations, what we know as *prejudice*, which is a preconceived hostility toward an individual based on group membership. When interacting with a client, you should not generally attribute negative characteristics to the client based on knowledge of or experience with a person or group with whom the client shares neutral affinities. Do not assume a negative characteristic about a client based on the client's membership in a group in one or more of whose members you have observed that negative characteristic.

For example, lawyers should avoid assuming that a client is poor, illiterate, unsophisticated, unqualified, unprepared, or unaware, or a substance abuser or violent, simply because of the client's ethnicity, age, sex, country of origin, demeanor, dress, or other affinities. Be especially aware of and take great care with your negative attributions. Pathological attribution is especially deleterious when doing so will inhibit your relationship with a client and make ineffective your counsel and advice. To attribute negative characteristics to a client based on neutral affinities may insult and offend the client, lead to the termination of the professional relationship, and result in a professional grievance, civil-rights complaint, and other adverse effect on your reputation, employment, and career.

Diversity Everywhere

Consider examples from a soup kitchen where lawyers provide pro bono legal service. You might expect that persons frequenting a soup kitchen are poor. In most cases, they are. Yet within that population, one can find great diversity in experience, education, vocation, and legal, financial, and business sophistication. Poor does not mean unlearned, unskilled, or unsophisticated. At the soup kitchen and nearby homeless mission, lawyers provide pro bono legal service to poor and poorly dressed clients who nonetheless hold active professional licenses, have earned substantial six-figure salaries, and hold Ph.D. degrees.

Lawyers have homeless and destitute clients conduct their own legal research, draft their own court papers, and conduct their own federal and state-court litigation. Lawyers have seen them form their own corporations, qualify them as tax exempt, file annual reports, and manage corporate affairs. Serious illness, divorce, depression, criminal conviction, and other challenges can take a person from wealth to poverty quickly, notwithstanding substantial expertise. Lawyers also represent wealthy owners of successful corporations who do not have a high-school education, have insignificant legal, financial, and management expertise, and could not do the administrative tasks that some homeless clients can do. Wealth is no sure indicator of expertise.

> "In respect of civil rights, common to all citizens, the constitution of the United States does not, I think, permit any public authority to know the race of those entitled to be protected in the enjoyment of such rights. Every true man has pride of race, and under appropriate circumstances, when the rights of others, his equals before the law, are not to be affected, it is his privilege to express such pride and to take such action based upon it as to him seems proper. But I deny that any legislative body or judicial tribunal may have regard to the race of citizens when the civil rights of those citizens are involved. Indeed, such legislation as that here in question is inconsistent not only with that equality of rights which pertains to citizenship, national and state, but with the personal liberty enjoyed by every one within the United States.
>
> "The thirteenth amendment does not permit the withholding or the deprivation of any right necessarily inhering in freedom. It not only struck down

the institution of slavery as previously existing in the United States, but it prevents the imposition of any burdens or disabilities that constitute badges of slavery or servitude. It decreed universal civil freedom in this country. This court has so adjudged. But, that amendment having been found inadequate to the protection of the rights of those who had been in slavery, it was followed by the fourteenth amendment, which added greatly to the dignity and glory of American citizenship, and to the security of personal liberty, by declaring that 'all persons born or naturalized in the United States, and subject to the jurisdiction thereof, are citizens of the United States and of the state wherein they reside,' and that 'no state shall make or enforce any law which shall abridge the privileges or immunities of citizens of the United States; nor shall any state deprive any person of life, liberty or property without due process of law, nor deny to any person within its jurisdiction the equal protection of the laws.' These two amendments, if enforced according to their true intent and meaning, will protect all the civil rights that pertain to freedom and citizenship. Finally, and to the end that no citizen should be denied, on account of his race, the privilege of participating in the political control of his country, it was declared by the fifteenth amendment that 'the right of citizens of the United States to vote shall not be denied or abridged by the United States or by any state on account of race, color or previous condition of servitude.'

"These notable additions to the fundamental law were welcomed by the friends of liberty throughout the world. They removed the race line from our governmental systems. ...

"The white race deems itself to be the dominant race in this country. And so it is, in prestige, in achievements, in education, in wealth, and in power. So, I doubt not, it will continue to be for all time, if it remains true to its great heritage, and holds fast to the principles of constitutional liberty. But in view of the constitution, in the eye of the law, there is in this country no superior, dominant, ruling class of citizens. There is no caste here. Our constitution is color-blind, and neither knows nor tolerates classes among citizens. In respect of civil rights, all citizens are equal before the law. The humblest is the peer of the most powerful. The law regards man as man, and takes no account of his surroundings or of his color when his civil rights as guaranteed by the supreme law of the land are involved. It is therefore to be regretted that this high tribunal, the final expositor of the fundamental law of the land, has reached the conclusion that it is competent for a state to regulate the enjoyment by citizens of their civil rights solely upon the basis of race.

"In my opinion, the judgment this day rendered will, in time, prove to be quite as pernicious as the decision made by this tribunal in the Dred Scott

Case."   Plessy v. Ferguson, 163 U.S. 537, 554-555, 559 (1896) (Harlan, J., dissenting).

Cultural Affinities

The professional skill of avoiding pathological attribution actually involves a delicate balance. On one hand, a lawyer should avoid pathological attribution. On the other hand, a lawyer should not overlook important affinities. Notice the tension. Individuals find society, comfort, identity, and meaning within culture. Sharing culture with another, even if it involves so little as the form of greeting, can provide important bonds and efficiencies. When lawyers share professional culture with other lawyers, they do not have to investigate, identify, and develop shared norms. They can speak and act without thought to the cultural form of their expression, trusting that the other lawyer will understand and respect the action without misinterpreting it.

Those who are not lawyers gain the same efficiencies when sharing culture with others. Two individuals who understand and share the same culture can greet one another, converse, and act without misunderstanding one another, by relying on their shared culture. Individuals who move in and out of different cultures, which includes many lawyers, adjust their behaviors to each culture. Lawyers learn to speak, think, and act one way among other lawyers, sharing professional culture, while acting a different way among family members, friends, or clients embracing other cultures.

In that respect, individuals do not genetically inherit culture, and culture does not fix itself permanently to an individual. Rather, first family relationships, and later social and work relationships and educational programs, develop multiple cultural affinities within individuals. Varied circumstances help some individuals both develop multiple cultural affinities and learn to adapt quickly to other cultures. More-stable, fixed circumstances help other individuals develop strong single cultural affinities and learn to draw heavily from that single culture. Most often, cultural acquisition and adaptation occurs subconsciously and intuitively.

Yet lawyers and others can learn to recognize cultural influences in order to adapt more quickly and effectively.

Multicultural Approaches

Multicultural means comprising, forming, or representing several different cultures. While American popular culture unifies the nation's inhabitants, American society is nonetheless multicultural. What passes for respect, humor, generosity, or kindness in one American subculture may not constitute the same message in another. Words and actions take on different meaning in different cultures. To be respectfully or even fashionably late in one subculture might be to disrespect one's waiting host in another subculture. To bring an appropriately generous gift in one subculture might be to disrespect the provision of one's host in another subculture.

Groups and individuals may also adopt multiple cultural identities. Individuals including lawyers who live or work across multicultural settings may consciously manipulate or unconsciously modify their own cultural identity back and forth across settings. Lawyers, clients, and others can readily develop and exhibit multiple cultural identities useful in different environments. A multicultural approach to professional skills would be to learn as many features of as many cultures and subcultures as possible, to adjust accordingly. Cross-cultural learning can be instructive and enjoyable. Immerse yourself in other cultures. Doing so will teach you their depth and subtleties. It will also teach you the depth and subtlety of your own culture.

Limitation on Multicultural Practices

As worthwhile as they can be, multicultural approaches to professional service can present their own challenges when accepted as the primary or sole framework for a lawyer's cross-cultural skills. First, the number of cultures and subcultures is endless. The world and even the country harbors dozens if not hundreds of Native American, African, European, Indian, Middle Eastern, Asian, Pacific Islander, and other subcultures. Culture varies too widely and distinct subcultures are too numerous to have any confidence that one has a sufficiently broad and deep grasp of them all to rely only on that cultural knowledge. We would not have time to learn enough of them.

Second, the markers for who operates within a certain culture are not always so clear. For example, just because a person wears African dress does not mean that they know and share African culture. On one hand, they may have been raised in Africa and thus have deep knowledge of and affinity for African culture, which in itself varies very widely. On the other hand, they may have just liked the look of African clothing designs, have never been to Africa, and have only superficial knowledge of African culture. For a lawyer to assume either deep cultural knowledge and affinity or the opposite could interfere with a productive professional relationship.

Even having been born and raised in a certain geographic region, or having spent substantial time there, does not mean that one knows or shares that region's culture. Families and other sub-groups isolate themselves within cultures, developing their own culture or adopting the culture of outside religions, societies, or sects. Lawyers who immerse themselves in different cultures may learn the norms and practices within those cultures, making them better able to communicate with and serve effectively clients who share that culture. Yet immersion in one culture does not necessarily prepare a lawyer for cross-cultural practice with members of other cultures or with individuals who do not share their home region's culture.

"Cross-cultural lawyering occurs when lawyers and clients have different ethnic or cultural heritages and when they are socialized by different subsets within ethnic groups. By this definition, everyone is multi-cultural to some degree. Cultural groups and cultural norms can be based on ethnicity, race, gender, nationality, age, economic status, social status, language, sexual orientation, physical characteristics, marital status, role in family, birth order, immigration status, religion, accent, skin color or a variety of other characteristics." Susan Bryant, *The Five Habits: Building Cross-Cultural Competence in Lawyers*, 8 CLIN. L. REV. 33, 41 (2001) (footnotes omitted).

Cognition as a Source of Bias

In addition to the large number of cultures and subcultures, and the challenge that learning enough about enough of them would present, multicultural frameworks present another challenge as a basis for cross-cultural professional practice. That challenge has to do with bias. *Bias* is an inherent inclination toward a conclusion that data would not necessarily support. Biases are unsupported pattern recognitions or, to put it more accurately, pattern *assumptions.* By definition, biases are unreliable if not always inaccurate. A bias may actually be consistent with unobserved data, or it may not, which is the point that biases involve inclinations without data support.

Although we tend to lump bias together with *prejudice,* treating them both as negatives, in strict connotation the two words have an important difference in their meaning. *Prejudice* assigns unsupported *negative* attributes to a person, having *negative* consequences to that person, while in its strict meaning *bias* may assign positive or negative attributes having positive or negative consequences. Your *bias* may be to always extend a warm hand of greeting even though in some situations doing so may not be warranted or appropriate. Your *prejudice* would deny that warm greeting to an individual of a certain class even though you should have extended it. Prejudice, a normative term to which we assign strong negative value, is a subset of bias, a value-free, scientific (criterion-based) term.

Surprising as it may seem, biases are actually useful in many instances, again if one understands bias to be distinct from *prejudice.* Although biases are by definition unreliable because not supported by data, biases create meaning for us nonetheless. Those meanings may be unsupported by data, but they are still capable of guiding our behavior. We make meaning out of situations and data by recognizing patterns. Whatever data that we have at hand, we naturally examine and sort with conscious effort and unconscious habit of mind. The data may be events, conditions, groups, or individual behaviors. As we observe that data, our powerful minds form patterns. Cognition constantly categorizes and assesses variation, making bias implicit in everything that we do.

Often, meaning is more important to individual comfort, vitality, initiative, action, survival, and prosperity than non-meaning. We often desire and sometimes need meaning over chaos, even when chaos is all that we have. Action, even when based on bias, is sometimes more important than inaction. Direction, even when based on inaccurate assumptions, is sometimes more important than lack of direction. Biases are natural, common, frequent, commonly helpful, probably necessary, and in themselves neutral. Recognizing that we all constantly operate on biases is an important first step toward recognizing and meeting the challenge of avoiding prejudices.

> "In order to make sense of and navigate the incredible volume of data that human beings encounter from day to day, human brains organize and categorize information into schemas—or mental shortcuts.
>
> "Implicit social cognitions are the schemas that apply to human interaction and that guide the way a person thinks about social categories. Social cognitions include stereotypes (traits we associate with a category) and attitudes (evaluative feelings that are positive or negative).
>
> "Implicit bias is a preference (positive or negative) for a group based on a stereotype or attitudes we hold and that tends to develop early in life. Implicit bias operates outside of human awareness and can be understood as a lens through which a person views the world and that automatically filters how a person takes in and acts in regard to information." American Bar Association, *Building Community Trust: Improving Cross-cultural Communication in the Criminal Justice System* 27 (June 2010).

Groups as Sources of Bias

Nearly all of us desire to belong to certain groups, whether Copts, Jews, Lutherans, tradespersons, homemakers, teenagers, Masons, Rotarians, Red Sox fans, Yankee fans, TJ Maxx shoppers, or lawyers. Affinities are powerful personal and professional resources. The identity of a group is another source of bias. We see meaning in groups to which we belong or others belong, even when the meaning is not entirely, not uniformly, or not at all there.

As you read the above list of groups, you probably made some associations with at least some of the categories. Indeed, others might well have judged you culturally unaware if you were unable to do so. One can think of associations and affinities as biases.

The desire to belong to groups is another source of bias. For example, lawyers may tend to appreciate the company, or at least the thought of the company, of other lawyers. In mixed groups, lawyers may stick together out of affinity for their fellow professionals. In one instance, a lawyer board member dissented to proposed action of a legal-information organization. The non-lawyer board members criticized, gossiped about, railed at, and disrespected the lawyer in a manner that lawyers would not tend to do to one another. They also criticized lawyers generally. The other lawyer board members came to the lawyer's defense, dividing the board along lawyer and non-lawyer lines. Each group, lawyer and non-lawyer, felt the need to defend the other members of their group. A group of any kind can be a source of bias.

Culture as a Source of Bias

Culture, or cultural metaphor, is itself another source of bias. Read, watch, or listen to any world news. The journalists and producers who identify what constitutes news and who report the news constantly use cultural metaphors. The news asserts broadly that homeowners buckle, farmers protest, Iranians rankle, Russians bolster, the elderly fret, the young boast, Catholics celebrate, nations conspire, and leaders dawdle, as if each group or category had cohesive interests, actions, and intent. Yet without those broad assertions that ignore unending variety within each such group or category, those who report and listen to the news would not be able to make of it any sense. Cultural metaphor undergirds an important system of making and communicating meaning. We deliberately understand events within broad cultural contexts that mask individual interests, actions, and variety.

"From Aunt Jemima advertisements to the board game Ghettopoly, American popular culture is replete with racist images. The Jim Crow Museum of Racist Memorabilia features an extensive collection of racist objects that trace the history of the stereotyping of African Americans. The museum, located at Ferris State University, is offering "Hateful Things," a traveling exhibition of these images to further the museum's mission of stimulating the scholarly examination of historical and contemporary expressions of racism, as well as promoting racial understanding and healing.

"In the early 1830s Thomas Dartmouth Rice created the antebellum character Jim Crow. 'Daddy Rice' was a white actor who performed, in blackface, a song-and-dance whose exaggerations popularized racially demeaning minstrel shows. The name 'Jim Crow' came to denote segregation in the 19th century when Southern and Border states passed 'Jim Crow laws,' legitimizing a racial caste system.

"The 39 piece traveling exhibition contains items of material culture from the late 19th century to the present, embodying the terrible effects of the Jim Crow legacy. In addition to items from popular and commercial culture, the traveling exhibit also contains images of violence against African Americans as well as the Civil Rights struggle for racial equality. ...

"The disturbing objects in 'Hateful Things' have been lifted from their original purposes to now serve as powerful reminders of America's racist past. But more importantly, the exhibition gives viewers new eyes with which to see present-day images of racial stereotyping that might otherwise pass unchallenged." Ferris State University Jim Crow Museum of Racist Memorabilia, http://www.ferris.edu/jimcrow/traveling/.

Balancing Bias

Lawyers must balance the powerful lens of cultural metaphor against the reality of individual client experience and service. Lawyers must keep cultural metaphor in just the right tension with the individual reality of the represented client. Lawyers must avoid carrying out a representation by relying on broad cultural assumptions when to the contrary *individual clients* decide the goals of representation, weigh its objectives, and influence its methods.

We encounter prejudice when a lawyer acts on a bias in a way that negatively affects a client or client interest. Lawyers must not allow cultural metaphors to affect clients negatively. Lawyers must be able to discern when cultural metaphor adversely affects clients or client interests. What lawyers need for their many encounters with unlike others is a set of cross-cultural skills that give context to cultural references, evaluate the effect of cultural metaphor, and minimize inaccurate attribution. Lawyers need a *framework* through which they can quickly discern key cultural touch-points of the specific client whom they counsel.

Reflections

Consider the following reflections on group-based attribution. Add these reflections to your journal. Find an acquaintance with whom to discuss these questions, or organize a group discussion, to broaden your view:

1. To what groups (racial, ethnic, cultural, spiritual, political, etc.) do you feel that you most belong? Rank those affinities in order from strongest to weakest regarding your identity. On what attribute or commitment do you base those affinities? Are the affinities positive, negative, or both? That is, do you draw strength and advantage from those affinities, or do they burden you in some respect, or both?

2. To what groups (racial, ethnic, cultural, spiritual, political, etc.) would others assume that you belong? What characteristics or commitments would others attribute to you, to place you within those groups? Are the affinities positive, negative, or both? That is, would others regard you more highly because of those affinities, or would others regard you less because of those affinities, or both?

3. How do the groups to which you feel you belong (your answer to 1 above) and the groups to which others would assign you (your answer to 2 above) differ? Why do they differ? What is it about you that appears to others that differs from how you regard yourself? Can you think of an instance when others mistakenly assigned you a group affinity that you did not hold? What was it (name, skin color, hairstyle, dress, residence, etc.) that made others assign that affinity to you? Why were they mistaken?

4. Can you think of an instance when you mistakenly assigned someone else to a group affinity (racial, ethnic, cultural, spiritual, political, etc.) that they did not hold? What attribute

(name, skin color, hairstyle, dress, residence, etc.) was it about them that made you mistakenly assign them to that group? How did you learn that you were mistaken? What affect did your mistake have, if any?

5. Listen to, view, or read the evening news today. What group attributions do you discern? How necessary were those attributions? How helpful were those attributions? How harmful might those attributions have been? Did the news identify one or more of your affinity groups? Did the news treat your affinity group fairly? Do you have the attribute or tendency that the news attributed to your affinity group?

6. With what affinity groups do you deal in your professional practice? Do you have clients who wish you to identify them with certain affinity groups? Why would a client wish you and others to identify them as a member of a certain affinity group? What advantage might accrue to the client?

7. Do you have clients who resist identification with certain affinity groups to which you or others might assign them? Why would a client resist assignment to a certain affinity group to which you or others might naturally assign them? What disadvantage might accrue to the client?

8. Think of a professional situation in which you might need to distinguish your client from an affinity group to which your client belongs or to which others would assign your client. Why would you distinguish your client from that group affinity or the attributes others would assign to the client based on that affinity? How would you do so?

9. Observe a professional setting such as a courtroom or conference. What affinities do you see the participants claiming? What affinities do you see the participants admitting? What affinities do you see the participants resisting? What affinities do you see participants assigning to others? How do those affinities influence the professional events? Do you discern any fairness or unfairness in the assigning and use of those affinities?

10. Identify group attributions on which you depend in your professional practice. How did you learn or acquire them? How do they help you in your practice? Are they fair in every instance? Are there aspects of unfairness in them, to certain individuals? Are they over-inclusive? Are they under-inclusive? Should you adjust them, now that you have reflected on them?

Chapter 3

Idiographic

"Wasn't Einstein a white guy?"

Forms of Diversity Training

The diversity expert conducting the training for the assembled professionals was projecting a slide on a screen. The slide had two boxes at the left of the screen. One box the expert had labeled "Black" and the other "White." Next to each box "Black" and "White" were five empty boxes. The expert began to fill in the empty boxes. The exercise, the lawyer surmised quickly, was going to be quite interesting.

The expert then explained that black culture has certain features and white culture other features. The expert then showed on the same slide five features of black culture and five features of white culture. Each feature appeared as one word on the slide next to either "Black" or "White." The expert was going to show the group differences between black and white cultures.

The expert explained that the first feature of black culture is that blacks are relational, while whites are materialistic. The words went up on the screen: "Black = relational," "White = materialistic." The second feature, the expert continued, was that blacks are giving and generous while whites are acquisitive, taking things rather than giving things away. Up went the words on the screen: "Black = relational + giving," "Whites = materialistic + acquisitive."

The expert added third and fourth features that blacks are other-centered while whites are self-centered and that blacks are caring while whites are indifferent. Up went the words on the screen: "Black = relational + giving + other-centered + caring," "Whites = materialistic + acquisitive + self-centered + indifferent."

The expert concluded that the last feature of black culture is that blacks are relativistic thinkers, flexible and seeing things in proportion to other things, like Einstein did with his brilliant theory of relativity, while whites are linear thinkers, inflexible, and mechanistic, like old-fashioned Newtonians. Up went the words on the screen: "Black = relational + giving + other-centered + caring + relativistic (Einstein)," "White = materialistic + acquisitive + self-centered + indifferent + linear (Newton)."

At this point the lawyer, uncomfortable at the diversity trainer's straight-faced portrayal of blacks as friendly, giving, sensitive, caring, and smart but whites as unfriendly, greedy, selfish, uncaring, and stupid, turned to the person seated next to him and asked in half-jest, "Hey, wasn't Einstein a white dude?" The lawyer's seatmate glowered back at the lawyer, not sharing the lawyer's humor. The seatmate refused to speak to the lawyer for the rest of the diversity training.

"High in the tower, where I sit above the loud complaining of the human sea, I know many souls that toss and whirl and pass, but none there are that intrigue me more than the Souls of White Folk.

"Of them I am singularly clairvoyant. I see in and through them. I view them from unusual points of vantage. Not as a foreigner do I come, for I am native, not foreign, bone of their thought and flesh of their language. Mine is not the knowledge of the traveler or the colonial composite of dear memories, words and wonder. Nor yet is my knowledge that which servants have of masters, or mass of class, or capitalist of artisan. Rather I see these souls undressed and from the back and side. I see the working of their entrails. I know their thoughts and they know that I know. This knowledge makes them now embarrassed, now furious. They deny my right to live and be and call me misbirth! My word is to them mere bitterness and my soul, pessimism. And yet as they preach and strut and shout and threaten, crouching as they clutch at rags of facts and fancies to hide their nakedness, they go twisting, flying by my tired eyes and I see them ever stripped,—ugly, human.

"The discovery of personal whiteness among the world's peoples is a very modern thing,—a nineteenth and twentieth century matter, indeed. The ancient world would have laughed at such a distinction. The Middle Age regarded skin color with mild curiosity; and even up into the eighteenth century we were hammering our national manikins into one, great, Universal Man, with fine frenzy which ignored color and race even more than birth. Today we have changed all that, and the world in a sudden, emotional conversion has discovered that it is white and by that token, wonderful!" W.E.B. DuBois, Darkwater—Voices from Within the Veil (Harcourt, Brace & Co. 1920) (excerpt from Chapter 2: The Souls of White Folk).

Labeling Culture

When attributing characteristics to cultures, one must take care not to perpetuate stereotypes as to members of the group whom the culture embraces or describes. To say that black culture or white culture is a certain way may come close to saying, or may be misunderstood as saying, that blacks and whites are certain ways.

The above diversity trainer's defense would have been that she was only talking about cultures, not racial or ethnic groups or individual members of racial or ethnic groups, even though she stated frequently that "whites are..." and "blacks are...," only sometimes including but other times omitting references to white and black *culture.* The difference between asserting that "black *culture* is..." and "*blacks are...*" is a fine distinction at best and, if any distinction, one that too many persons would miss. The diversity expert had missed that subtlety several times in her own presentation when speaking of "blacks" and "whites" rather than "black culture" and "white culture." Indeed, her graphic projected on the big screen for all to see had stated simply "Black" and "White," not black *culture* and white *culture.*

Describing the culture of specific racial or ethnic groups while trying not to imply those cultural attributes to the groups' members is not even logical. A reasonable person could conclude that if the culture has the attribute, then so too should most of the members of the group embracing the culture. Lawyers should be careful when attributing characteristics to cultures, lest they attribute characteristics to clients who, though they associate with that culture, do not share those characteristics.

Exalting Culture

Lawyers should also appreciate the genuine interest that a diversity trainer would have in lauding the cultural propensities of her own ethnic group "Black" as she presented it. Lawyers can think generously of others, both groups and individuals. Thinking well of any group or individual can serve that group or individual and others who share the group or individual interest. Appreciating aspects of different cultures encourages us to explore and embrace other cultures. Appreciating other cultures may even cause lawyers to extend professional services to those who identify with the other cultures.

On the other hand, for a lawyer to attribute positive or negative characteristics to a client based on the client's identification with a certain cultural group, without evidence that the client actually possesses that characteristic, could prove problematic to the professional service. Lawyers should think of clients both with the generosity and candor necessary to effective professional service. Just because black culture may (as the trainer urged) be relational, giving, other-centered, caring, and relativistic does not mean that any particular client shares those attributes. The lawyer who assumes that any client shares attributes (positive, negative, or neutral) when the client does *not* share attributes may misconstrue the client's goals, interests, and preferences, and fail to advise and serve the client effectively.

Denigrating Culture

Another problem arises that while lauding cultural attributes of one group, in the above case "Blacks," a person might well disparage cultural propensities of other groups, in the above case "Whites." What the diversity trainer had depicted of white culture, particularly the materialism, acquisitiveness, self-interestedness, and indifference to others, could look to some like an unfortunately denigrating caricature or stereotype of Caucasian Americans. Once we accept the practice of describing cultures in laudatory ways, then we might too easily accept the practice of describing cultures in negative ways. Positive stereotypes can turn too easily to negative stereotypes. Negative stereotypes do not advance the willingness of one cultural group and individual members of it to think positively of and interact effectively with members of another cultural group.

Moreover, just because a certain culture may have negative attributes does not mean that a client whose affinity is for that cultural group will share those negative attributes. The lawyer who assumes that a client shares those negative attributes when the client does *not* share those attributes may misconstrue the client's goals, propose the wrong objectives, and fail to advise and serve the client effectively. To attribute features to culture and then assume that persons within that culture have that feature can be problematic in other ways. Doing so may insult and offend the client, lead to the termination of the professional relationship, and result in a professional grievance, civil-rights complaint, and other adverse effect on the lawyer's reputation, employment, and career.

"We come then to the question presented: Does segregation of children in public schools solely on the basis of race... deprive the children of the minority group of equal educational opportunities? We believe that it does.

"... The effect of this separation on their educational opportunities was well stated by a finding in the Kansas case by a court which nevertheless felt compelled to rule against the Negro plaintiffs: 'Segregation of white and colored children in public schools has a detrimental effect upon the colored children. The impact is greater when it has the sanction of the law; for the policy of separating the races is usually interpreted as denoting the inferiority of the negro group. A sense of inferiority affects the motivation of a child to learn. Segregation with the sanction of law, therefore, has a tendency to [retard] the educational and mental development of negro children and to deprive them of some of the benefits they would receive in a racial[ly] integrated school system.'

"We conclude that in the field of public education the doctrine of 'separate but equal' has no place. Separate educational facilities are inherently unequal. Therefore, we hold that the plaintiffs and others similarly situated for whom the actions have been brought are, by reason of the segregation complained of, deprived of the equal protection of the laws guaranteed by the Fourteenth

45

Amendment." Brown v. Board of Educ., 347 U.S. 483, 493-495 (1954) (opinion by Chief Justice Warren) (footnote omitted).

Distinguishing Culture

Consider an example. A Hispanic-Latino client met with the lawyer at the homeless mission, bringing a Hispanic-Latino friend to translate. The friend explained that as part of their cultural machismo, Hispanic-Latino men are generous to a fault with their children. His friend had been giving plenty of money to the mother of his children to care for his children.

"He buys the children food and new clothes, and even pays the mother's rent," the friend explained as the client smiled and nodded in agreement. "That's the way we Hispanic males are, macho, you know?" the friend added, as the client pulled from his wallet photographs of the well-dressed children to show the lawyer.

The friend then explained that the problem was that the mother was not letting the client see the children, alleging that the client had physically abused the mother in front of the children.

"We are rough with our women sometimes," the friend explained, referring to their Hispanic-Latino machismo while striking an intentionally comical pose of manly attitude, "But my friend, he's not that way. He's a gentle man."

With those last words about gentleness, the friend looked at the client, and they both laughed at the comically unmanly inference.

The lawyer did not diminish the friend and client's Hispanic-Latino cultural affinity in any respect. Instead, the lawyer joined in their laughter, sharing the repartee built around the friend's discussion of ethnic or cultural characteristics. Yet the lawyer also carefully avoided crediting or discrediting what the friend had said about Hispanic-Latino males and instead considered the facts that the friend had stated and implied about the client. The consultation ensued based on those specific attributions rather than assumptions based on the client's ethnic or cultural affinity.

The lawyer neither endorsed nor contradicted the friend's ethnic or cultural attributions. The lawyer did not agree that Hispanic-Latino males are good providers but rough with women. Others may not share those assessments, but in this consultation the lawyer would neither credit nor discredit them. The lawyer knew that assumptions about the client based on the client's cultural affinity could be hazardous in these circumstances. Domestic violence knows no cultural bounds. Neither does its absence. The client either was or was not a fit father. The case should turn on the credibility of the father's and witnesses' contentions, not on cultural presumptions.

"[Olga M.] Pina, the practice leader for international business at Fowler White Boggs in Tampa, Fla., spoke on an American Bar Association Annual Meeting Section of Litigation panel about the need for international lawyers to be alert to differing cultures and customs. Pina counsels her younger associates who work with foreign clients or overseas that a lawyer's appearance is as important as knowledge of the law, advocacy abilities and negotiating skills.

"'Most jurisdictions outside the U.S. don't do business casual,' Pina said. 'How you come across not only shows a sign of respect in your business, but it also sends a message about authority and power.'

"Pina observed that women lawyers in a professional setting have more flexibility in how they dress when dealing with Latin American cultures than they do in most Asian cultures, where dark, conservative suits are the norm. Language is another crucial consideration in conducting cross-border legal business, Pina said. When relying on translators, she said, it's important to make sure they are fluent not only in the foreign language, but also in the jurisdiction's laws and legal customs. Otherwise, misunderstandings can result." Ira Pilchen, *Cross-Cultural Legal Transactions Can Easily Get Lost in Translation* (ABA Aug. 5, 2011).

Attribution's Value

Attribution as to specific client characteristics can still be an important and powerful tool for a professional who serves diverse clients. To evaluate matters accurately, give effective advice, and take effective action, lawyers can benefit from knowing their

47

client's experiences, beliefs, habits, propensities, preferences, and characteristics. The challenge is to make accurate and neutral attributions that aid the professional service.

In the above instance, the lawyer needed to learn quickly what he could about the silent Hispanic-Latino client. The lawyer listened carefully to the friend throughout the brief consultation but watched *the client*'s movements and reactions to his friend's descriptions, drawing fair inferences from those observations. The client appeared to care for himself adequately in grooming and dress yet wore no expensive clothing or jewelry. He listened attentively and appeared to understand the English that his friend and the lawyer spoke, although he preferred to speak to his friend in Spanish.

The lawyer learned from the friend that the client was undocumented but working extra hours as a reliable employee in a steady business. The lawyer inferred that the client had the equivalent of a high school education. His goal, the lawyer easily discerned, was to reunite with his children's mother, who was a lawful resident alien, to best care for his children. The lawyer's attributions helped the lawyer determine achievable objections that would accomplish the client's goal.

The assertions that the friend had made and with which the client had agreed about the attributes of Hispanic-Latino men with respect to women and children had no bearing on the lawyer's assessment. That cultural context had nonetheless been the basis for a natural, warmly humorous communication that had established helpful rapport, trust, and confidence. The friend had used cultural knowledge and affinity to both *confirm* the client's attributes and to *distinguish* them, while the lawyer had avoided misattributions altogether without rejecting the cultural assertions and understandings of client and friend.

Jargon Warning

Here comes the jargon again. Follow it just long enough to get the gist of the involved skills. Then forget the jargon while remembering the skills. Simply understand for now a precise

48

term for a fundamental practice that can promote effective cross-cultural legal service.

Idiographic Attribution

Idio is a prefix or combining form having the connotation or meaning of being unique to an individual, specific to one, or peculiar as to that person. For example, an *idio*m is an expression peculiar to a specific group or language that others would misunderstand from its literal meaning. For another example, *idio*syncratic means peculiar and unpredictable, after the fashion of one. Then, *graphic* means to describe a condition, give a clear picture of something, or show by diagram. Thus, *idiographic* means to give a clear picture of one condition, to describe specifics of an individual situation, or to make a case study of one person. Idiographic is the opposite of *nomothetic*, which is to derive general observations of personality traits.

Idiographic attribution then means to attribute habits, behaviors, or characteristics to one person based on a case study of that person. As the above example of the Hispanic-Latino male client demonstrates, idiographic attribution is a lawyer's foundational cross-cultural skill. The client's actual characteristics and circumstances were both like and unlike other Hispanic-Latino males' characteristics and circumstances, as the friend described those cultural assumptions. Because the lawyer took care to ascertain the client's specific characteristics and circumstances through *idiographic* rather than *pathological* attribution, the cross-cultural consultation worked well.

"… If we shall suppose that American slavery is one of those offenses which, in the providence of God, must needs come, but which, having continued through His appointed time, he now wills to remove, and that he gives to both North and South this terrible war, as the woe due to those by whom the offense came, shall we discern therein any departure from those divine attributes which the believers in a living God always ascribe to him?

"Fondly do we hope, fervently do we pray, that this mighty scourge of war may speedily pass away. Yet, if God wills that it continue until all the wealth piled by the bondsman's two hundred and fifty years of unrequited toil shall be sunk, and until every drop of blood drawn with the lash shall be paid by another drawn with the sword, as was said three thousand years ago, so still it must be said, 'The judgments of the Lord are true and righteous altogether.'

"With malice toward none; with charity for all; with firmness in the right, as God gives us to see the right, let us strive on to finish the work we are in; to bind up the nation's wounds; to care for him who shall have borne the battle and for his widow, and his orphan—to do all which may achieve and cherish a just and lasting peace among ourselves, and with all nations." Abraham Lincoln, *Second Inaugural Address* (1865), in WILLIAM O. DOUGLAS, MR. LINCOLN & THE NEGROES: THE LONG ROAD TO EQUALITY 122-23 (Atheneum 1963).

Building Idiographic Client Models

Idiographic attribution is important in all lawyer-client relationships, not just when serving foreign or discrete populations. Lawyers represent well-dressed and well-educated clients who are nonetheless poor, victimized, without social support, and without other resources, perhaps because of domestic violence, severe illness, job loss, or other isolation. Contrarily, lawyers represent poorly dressed and apparently uneducated clients who are nonetheless of means and who have strong social support and other resources. Pay careful attention to the client's specific attributes and condition, without unsupported assumptions, while recognizing and respecting the client's social and cultural context.

Lawyers can embrace social and cultural context, and appreciate multicultural context. They just have to have the skills to build an idiographic model of each client within those cultural and social contexts. One of those skills is idiographic attribution, which enables lawyers to engage and respect culture while recognizing the unique experience and appreciating the unique presentation of each client. Culture and individuality meet within idiographic attribution. Lawyers give clients the best opportunity for effective legal service when the lawyer builds a socio-cultural model for each individual client out of idiographic attributions within the client's expressed cultural context.

The lawyer serving the Hispanic-Latino male client in the above example made idiographic attributions as to the client's legal status, earnings, education, and commitments, while setting that idiographic client model within the Hispanic-Latino cultural and social identity that the client and his friend so readily communicated and embraced. The client had chosen his own commitments and built his own meaning within a strong cultural identity that on the one hand supported his embrace of mother and children, and his responsibility to provide for them, but on the other hand challenged the client's individual commitment to treat mother respectfully and gently.

Study shows the value of attribution theory. Indeed, each of us constructs cognitive *self*-schemas, meaning generalizations that we make constantly about ourselves, from diverse social and cultural influences. We also construct self-schema out of core commitments that may be quite unlike those social and cultural influences. Then, whenever relating to others, we construct schemas of those others. The skill for lawyers is to construct client schemas accurately, positively, and productively for effective legal service. Idiographic models help lawyers do so. You will soon have a more-detailed framework within which to make idiographic attributions. First, though, consider in the next chapter some history of diversity-and-inclusion theory.

Reflections

Consider the following reflections on idiographic attribution. Add these reflections to your journal. Find an acquaintance with whom to discuss these questions, or organize a group discussion, to broaden your view:

1. Choose the affinity group (social, recreational, political, ethnic, spiritual, etc.) with which you most closely identify. What attributes do you have or commitments do you hold that distinguish you from the group, despite your affinity?

2. Is there any affinity group to which you belong, few or none of which its common attributes or commitments you share? Why do you belong to that group nonetheless? How do other members of the group regard your distinctions, or how would they regard them if they knew of them? Do those distinctions make you any less a member of the affinity group?

3. Choose an affinity-group member whom you know well. Now name some attributes or commitments of that individual that differ from the other members of the affinity group of which that person is a member. How important do you think it is to that person that you are aware of that person's distinction from the affinity group in those respects?

4. Identify an attribute you have or commitment you hold, and then identify three different affinity groups that, though different, nonetheless tend to share that attribute or commitment.

5. Now, identify a second attribute you have or commitment you hold that clearly distinguishes you from at least one of those three affinity groups that you identified in your prior answer.

6. Now, identify a third attribute you have or commitment you hold that distinguishes you from all three of the affinity groups that you identified in your prior answer.

7. Identify a constellation of attributes you have or commitments you hold (an idiographic model) that you believe distinguishes you from every other person, that is, that makes you unique.

8. Choose a person whom you know well. Identify attributes that person has or commitments that person holds that, collectively, distinguish that person from every other person, that is, that make that person unique. How did you get to know that person well enough to construct that unique idiographic model?

9. Identify three affinity groups to which the person you identified in your prior answer belongs. For each such group, identify an attribute the person has or a commitment the person holds that distinguishes the person from the group you identified.

10. Identify a major ethnic, racial, political, spiritual, or cultural group. Articulate for that group the two most common attributes that a majority of its members may have or two most common commitments that a majority of its members may hold. Now, identify a member of that group that does not have each such attribute or hold each such commitment. Do you believe that some persons would presume that member to have those

common attributes or hold those common commitments, even though that member does not?

Chapter 4

Historical

"Get down on the floor!"

Histories of Conflict

History influences culture. The collective experience that history represents shapes culture much as personal experience influences personal behavior. History includes conflict. Because history influences culture and history includes conflict, conflict influences culture. All is not rosy in the matter of culture, which inevitably includes substantial historical conflict and tension. Lawyers can benefit from knowing histories of conflict, when attempting to understand client goals, behaviors, and expectations influenced by culture.

Consider an example. The mother and two young children waited in the car parked along the side of the urban street as the father went up to his office to get some work papers. Strangely, large crowds of African-American residents churned angrily at each nearby intersection in the sweltering summer heat. The anxious mother cursed under her breath at her husband's delay. They should have been safely on their way home by now, indeed, never should have been waiting unattended in the car on the street outside the husband's office.

Suddenly a young African-American man ran up beside the car, stopping just long enough to dart down an alley next to the office building. The mother looked with alarm from her front passenger seat down the alley in the direction that the young man had just run.

Seconds later, a white police officer ran up to the same spot next to the car, stopped, drew his gun, aimed at the fleeing youth, and fired two shots in the youth's direction down the alley. Neither the mother nor the children staring out the car's back window could quite see whether the officer had shot the youth. The mother was not waiting to find out. Uttering an expletive that neither child would forget, she threw herself over the back of her front seat to push her children down to the floor of the car, holding herself over them until her unsuspecting husband returned to the car a few minutes later.

The frightened family needed hours to navigate the crowded streets for the 10-minute trip home. Police had closed the interstate to frustrate snipers from using the overpasses to shoot at cars. Crowds jammed the urban streets. Looters broke windows and set cars on fire. National Guard vehicles sat at neighborhood intersections with personnel seated at turret-mounted machine guns in the back. In the next five days, riots traced to racial tensions over law-enforcement abuses, housing inequality, and other conflict in the city would kill 43, injure 1,100, and incarcerate 7,000. The children slept with buckets of water in their bedroom in case of firebombs.

> "Today the majority of South Africans, black and white, recognize that apartheid has no future. It has to be ended by our own decisive mass action in order to build peace and security. The mass campaign of defiance and other actions of our organization and people can only culminate in the establishment of democracy. The destruction caused by apartheid on our sub-continent is incalculable. The fabric of family life of millions of my people has been shattered. Millions are homeless and unemployed. Our economy lies in ruins and our people are embroiled in political strife. Our resort to the armed struggle in 1960 with the formation of the military wing of the ANC, Umkhonto we Sizwe, was a purely defensive action against the violence of apartheid. The factors which necessitated the armed struggle still exist today. We have no option but to continue. We express the hope that a climate conducive to a negotiated settlement will be created soon so that there may no longer be the need for the armed struggle." Nelson Mandela, *Speech on Release from Prison* (February 11, 1990).

History of Diversity Education

The effort to help lawyers and other professionals acquire greater skill in serving diverse populations has its own history. You may understand the concepts in this book and acquire cross-cultural skills more readily if you know some of that history of diversity education.

Diversity instruction began by stressing the different experiences of members of differently situated groups. Membership in an African-American, Caucasian-American, Hispanic-Latino, or other ethnic, racial, or socio-cultural group defined the instructional goals for members of each group. This early form of diversity education assumed that group members had similar experiences that diversity instruction then needed to communicate to members of other groups presumed not to have had those experiences. Diversity instruction would show that group members either shared or lacked resources in ways different from members of other groups whom the instruction presumed were unaware of those differences.

Early diversity education thus took a group-based, us-them, binary approach to instruction. Diversity educators instructed that groups in some cases had claims and causes against other groups, making perpetrators out of some groups and victims out of other groups. Some groups required validation or celebration. Other groups required condemnation, confession, and remediation. These binary approaches to diversity education have value and serve legitimate instructional goals. They have particular value around increasing individual awareness of the variety of human experience within different groups and the conflict that can arise out of those different experiences.

On the other hand, group-based approaches to diversity education can occasionally foster greater conflict than is productive, leading to participant disengagement from and rejection of the education. The effect of group-based approaches can also vary widely with the quality of instruction and with the makeup and dynamics of different groups and their commitments. Moreover, a group-based, binary approach, while increasing awareness, does not necessarily equip a lawyer with affirmative skills to serve a diverse population. While sensitizing lawyers, the binary approach does not necessarily provide a holistic, flexible, and practical framework within which lawyers can exercise sensitive cross-cultural skills.

"Following negotiations between the Boyd County High School Gay Straight Alliance and the Board of Education of Boyd County, Kentucky, the board ... agreed to implement mandatory staff and student diversity training that would address issues of sexual orientation and gender harassment. As part of the training, students in the middle and high schools were shown age-appropriate, hour-long antiharassment videos with follow-up comments from an instructor. Following the presentation, students had the opportunity to ask questions and were given blank comment cards where they could express their reactions to the video. Just before the training began at the high school, the plaintiffs' parents and several other parents submitted homemade 'opt-out'"notices to the school; their children did not attend, and as a result received unexcused absences.

"Plaintiffs sued alleging that by forcing students to attend mandatory diversity training that promotes a respectful coexistence with homosexuals, the school violated their constitutional rights of free speech and free exercise of religion. Additionally, several parents claimed the mandatory diversity training interfered with their right to direct their children's religious and ideological upbringing. The United States District Court for the Eastern District of Kentucky held that the diversity training did not violate any student's First Amendment rights. The court reasoned that the only restrictions placed on student speech related to disruptive harassment, and the training did not compel students to endorse or disavow any religious or moral beliefs relating to homosexuality. Furthermore, the court held that because the training was reasonably related to school safety, parents did not have the right to dictate how the school functioned." J. Colin Heffernan, Morrison ex rel. Morrison v. Board of Education: *A Road Map to Constitutional Diversity Training in Schools*, 16 LAW & SEXUALITY 145 (2007) (footnotes omitted).

Critical Approaches

The traditional group-based approach to diversity education soon paved the way for newer structural approaches in which diversity scholars developed structural critiques of institutions. In a structural critique, individual behaviors are less important because they are less likely to affect large numbers while also being harder to identify and change. A single person harboring prejudice may do less damage, be harder to discover, and be unlikely to change. Identifying and changing the attitude of one person may also make little difference if the institutions within which the person operates maintain prejudicial policies and practices.

By contrast, institutional policies and practices are more important as more likely to affect large numbers. Institutional practices are also easier to identify and possibly easier to change, particularly through education and legal action. Change the institution, and individuals will change with it. Individuals who have already changed will find the institutional support they need to carry out their best intentions.

Institutions subject to critique included education, employment, healthcare, land use, justice systems, government, law enforcement, marriage, the family, and any number of other social systems. Indeed, every institution is subject to structural critique, even the scholarship of diversity education, exactly as attempted here. Structural critiques evaluated how those institutions differently affected groups defined by race, ethnicity, national origin, language, gender, age, family or marital status, disability, physical appearance, occupation, and other characteristics. Any characteristic could define a group for purposes of structural critique.

Structural critiques have been greatly valuable in identifying and correcting prejudicial policies and practices of institutions. They will continue to prove valuable in an ever-wider array of institutional studies. Yet although valuable, the structural approach can occasionally engender alienation from the means by which individuals might most usefully affect change. Identifying institutional policies that have disparate impact may discourage individuals from resorting to the very institutions they most need. Law-enforcement practices reflect structural issues, but those most likely to benefit from structural reforms may also be those most in need of law-enforcement protection.

Moreover, structural approaches do not necessarily aid individual lawyers interested in offering more-effective cross-cultural service to individual clients. The lawyer who through structural critiques is aware of institutional biases may work to change the institution. Yet the goal of individual service is to help the individual, not change the institution. Communicating to the individual client that the institutions with which the client must deal have particular biases may not even help and may instead discourage or frustrate the client. Lawyers need an individualized framework within which to maximize the effectiveness of their cross-cultural service.

> "Even if Critical legal theory accepts the subjectivist critiques of the more determinist variants of Marxism, the implications of those structuralist forms of analysis remain deeply embedded within its argument. Most importantly, Critical thought incorporates the structuralist theory of the subject as an artifact produced by the cultural subsystem associated with an underlying economic conjuncture, and rejects the liberal image of the autonomy of consciousness. This structuralist position, beyond its Marxist or materialist formulation, is put more generally by Foucault: 'The individual is not to be conceived as a sort of elementary nucleus, a primitive atom, a multiple and inert material on which power comes to fasten or against which it happens to strike, and in so doing subdues or crushes individuals. In fact, it is already one of the prime effects of power that certain bodies, certain gestures, certain discourses, certain desires come to be identified and constituted as individuals. The individual, that is, is not the *vis-à-vis* of power; it is, I believe, one of its prime effects.'
>
> "For structuralism, then, individuality is a surface appearance that manifests the illusion that one existentially creates an identity-an identity actually produced by the encounter between human potentiality and the social constellations represented in, for example, language, myth, ideology, and law." Thomas C. Heller, *Structuralism and Critique*, 36 STAN. L.REV. 127, 131 (1984) (footnotes omitted).

Inter-Subjective Approaches

Today, diversity instruction tends toward *inter-subjective* approaches. An inter-subjective approach is one that recognizes that every individual has an individual experience, the telling of which can build relationship and community. *Inter* means between, in this case between two or more individuals. *Subjective* means peculiar to the individual or as seen by that individual. *Inter-subjective* thus implies two or more individuals sharing individual stories out of which they build common goals and understanding.

Inter-subjective approaches recognize that the individual experience of an African American may be different from the individual experience of a Caucasian American or Hispanic Latino. Yet more so, inter-subjective approaches recognize that the individual experience of an African American may be quite unlike relatively common experiences of other African Americans. Likewise, the individual experience of a Caucasian American or Hispanic Latino may be unlike relatively common experiences of other members of the same group.

Inter-subjective approaches do not diminish the significance of group membership. Rather, the commonality or individuality of the individual's experiences as an African American or Caucasian American itself becomes a part of the story that an individual shares with others, through which individuals build a community of interests. Every individual both faces challenges and celebrates victories. Every individual also has advantages within certain cultural contexts and disadvantages within others. In the inter-subjective approach, we are all both perpetrators in some instances and victims in other instances, each in unique ways some of which we share with our affinity group and others of which we do not share with our affinity group.

The goal of inter-subjective approaches is to increase the skill of each individual at identifying meaningful experiences and affinities through communication with others. Lawyer and client relate not through membership or non-membership in groups, and not through awareness of structural deficiencies, but through sensitive interaction building shared commitments and truth. The value to a lawyer of inter-subjective approaches is that they require the lawyer to listen to, observe, and communicate with each client in ways that construct individual understanding and connection. Among the three successive forms of diversity education, inter-subjectivity is the most appropriate approach around which to build a framework for professional service.

> "The exercise of judgment in legal decision-making and problem-solving is inherently complex, requiring the lawyer to draw on a multiplicity of intellectual capacities. Although central to lawyering, the development of independent professional judgment is not given appreciable attention in the conventional law school curriculum. Indeed, focusing almost exclusively on rule-based inductive, deductive, and categorical reasoning processes and linguistic precision, traditional law school pedagogy neglects other kinds of intellectual activity such as narrative, interpersonal, intrapersonal, and strategizing work, all of which are essential to the exercise of sound legal judgment. This disproportionate privileging of some lawyering intelligences over other equally important ones has been shown to effectively desensitize law students to personal and structural concerns that are critical to the sort of broad-gauged, contextualized, and morally nuanced judgment that is the hallmark of ethical and socially responsible lawyering." Angela O. Burton, *Cultivating Ethical, Socially Responsible Lawyer Judgment: Introducing the Multiple Lawyering Intelligences Paradigm into the Clinical Setting*, 11 Clinical L. Rev. 15, 17 (2004).

Reflections

Consider the following reflections on diversity-training approaches. Add these reflections to your journal. Find an acquaintance with whom to discuss these questions, or organize a group discussion, to broaden and enrich your view:

1. Identify a historical event (something that others would recognize) that you feel influenced your views and sensitivities about cross-cultural understanding. Why was that event significant to you? What did you learn from it regarding cross-cultural understanding? How has your view of the event changed over time? Do others hold different views of the same event? How do those views differ? Why do they differ?

2. Identify a personal event (something that others do not widely share) that you feel influenced you about cross-cultural understanding. Why was that event significant to you? What did you learn from it regarding cross-cultural understanding? How has your view of the event changed over time?

3. Have you been involved in cross-cultural conflict of any kind? What affinities (racial, ethnic, socioeconomic class, religious, national, etc.) defined the conflict's sides? How (by words, actions, attitudes, alliances, etc.) did participants express the conflict? What was the conflict's immediate source? What was the conflict's root cause? What was the conflict's resolution? What was the conflict's long-term effect or result? How did the different cultures of the participants influence their actions during the conflict?

4. Identify two groups to which you belong that give you an advantage over others who are not members of that group. Make one of your affinities based on an attribute over which you have no control and the other over an attribute or commitment that you do control. What are your advantages? Are they due you? Ought they to exist? How do non-members regard your advantages, as due to you or not due you? Could an initiative remove the advantages? If so, then by what process?

5. Now, identify two groups to which you belong that disadvantage you relative to others who are not members of that group. Again, as in your prior answer, make one of your affinities based on an attribute over which you have no control and the other over an attribute or commitment that you do control. What are your disadvantages? Are they due you? Ought they to exist? How do non-members regard your disadvantages, as due to you or not due you? Could an initiative remove the disadvantages? If so, then by what process?

6. Now, identify a single group to which you belong that carries both advantages and disadvantages relative to non-members of that group. What are the advantages? What are the disadvantages?

7. Find someone with whom to do these last exercises. Ask the other person to tell you about an advantage that they held over other members of a group to which they belonged (persons with whom they graduated from high school, residents of their neighborhood, applicants to their graduate program, etc.) that enabled them to achieve something not achieved by other

members of the group. How fair was that advantage? How did that advantage accrue to them? Was it something that they earned, something given to them, or something attributed to them? How did they feel about taking that advantage? How do they think that others felt about not having had that advantage?

8. Now, ask the other person to tell you about a disadvantage that they had over other members of a group to which they belonged that kept them from achieving or doing something that other members of the group were able to achieve or do. How fair was that disadvantage? How did that disadvantage accrue to them? Was it something that they failed to earn, something taken from them, or something attributed to them? How did they feel about not having that advantage?

9. Could you tell similar stories like those in the prior two answers?

Chapter 5

Subjective

"Another old white guy in a suit!"

Holding Viewpoints

The lawyer host finished introducing the next speaker. He sat down at one of the guest tables with other lawyers who were attending the state bar diversity conference.

"Oh, great," the younger female lawyer seated next to him said to no one in particular, rolling her eyes and making a look of disgust, "Do we have to hear from another old white guy in a suit?"

The lawyer host looked down at his old white hands, adjusting the sleeve of his suit while pretending to ignore the racial, sexual, age-related, and professional-dress-related insult.

The next speaker, though an older white male in a suit, was an award-winning national advocate for diversifying the profession. He sat by appointment on a national committee working to create greater opportunities within the profession for lawyers of diverse ethnicity. The speaker was to talk about a groundbreaking study he had published that should lead to greater diversity within the profession. He had given hundreds of hours of his professional career to supporting law students of diversity and to promoting diversity within the profession.

The attendees should hear from him, the host thought silently, just as the attendees had heard or would hear from one other old white guy in a suit, two younger black female lawyers, a black male lawyer, a Hispanic-Latino lawyer, and a black non-lawyer at the diversity conference. He hoped that the younger female lawyer could listen to each speaker, notwithstanding his or her sex, age, race, and professional dress.

> "I am in Birmingham because injustice is here. Just as the eighth-century prophets left their little villages and carried their "thus saith the Lord" far beyond the boundaries of their hometowns; and just as the Apostle Paul left his little village of Tarsus and carried the gospel of Jesus Christ to practically every hamlet and city of the Greco-Roman world, I too am compelled to carry the gospel of freedom beyond my particular hometown. Like Paul, I must constantly respond to the Macedonian call for aid.
>
> "Moreover, I am cognizant of the interrelatedness of all communities and states. I cannot sit idly by in Atlanta and not be concerned about what happens in Birmingham. Injustice anywhere is a threat to justice everywhere. We are caught in an inescapable network of mutuality, tied in a single garment of destiny. Whatever affects one directly affects all indirectly. Never again can we afford to live with the narrow, provincial "outside agitator" idea. Anyone who lives inside the United States can never be considered an outsider." Dr. Martin Luther King Jr., *Letter from Birmingham Jail* (August 1963).

Viewpoint Subjectivity

We all have cultural viewpoints. We each have a lens through which we view people, circumstances, and events. We each acquire that lens from the culture within which we operate. We each also modify that lens through a combination of our experiences, education, calling, and commitments.

The cultural lens through which we discern and interpret events can be a powerful ally and attribute. We would be lost without our cultural framework. That framework helps us construct meaning out of observations, without elaborate processing. The framework creates shorthand through which we read and interpret events more efficiently than we could without it.

The professional culture of a lawyer, particularly, provides a powerful interpretive framework for conditions and events. By intense training, lawyers develop ways of thinking, seeing, and speaking. They share sets of expectations. The frameworks of professional culture can be quite effective in addressing needs. Yet similarly, the perspective of one growing up in the inner city, on a farm, or in the South can provide a powerful lens through which to discern truth. No one cultural viewpoint necessarily has greater value in discerning truth than another cultural viewpoint.

Conflicting Viewpoints

Consider a relevant example of viewpoint subjectivity. Lawyers tend to see law as relatively rational (logical), largely normative (reflecting profound shared commitments), and primarily discrete (applying in specific settings). Many lawyers have few personal interactions with the law (relatively few personal legal matters). When those interactions occur, they tend to resolve fairly and meaningfully, reinforcing the lawyer's professional viewpoint.

By contrast, some clients experience the law and its enforcement in an opposite manner, as largely arbitrary, lacking in normative content, and omnipresent rather than compartmentalized and discrete. They may live in an environment where the justice and law-enforcement systems so seldom recognize and enforce personal rights, and legal representation is so unavailable, expensive, or ineffective, that the law reasonably appears to be arbitrary. Law operate with direct effect in nearly every aspect of their lives, whether as to family-law orders, legal documentation required for residence and employment, charges of crime and the collateral civil effects of conviction, legal effects of bad credit, or the availability of public benefits.

Reasonable viewpoints of the same legal service or justice system can vary widely, depending on personal position and circumstance. Simply because lawyers tend to have one perspective of the legal system does not mean that a particular client's quite-different perspective is not valid and reliable under the circumstances of that client. The lawyer's new presence in the client's life may soon change the validity and reliability of the client's perspective, but that change would depend on the lawyer's advice and actions and the client's willingness and ability to accept and benefit from them.

The Value of Viewpoint Variance

The value of those different cultural lenses is one reason why, at diversity conferences and in other places, we seek to present a range of speakers having different cultural viewpoints. The young female lawyer's frustration at hearing from two consecutive older white males in suits likely represented her desire to hear from other viewpoints. Race, sex, age, and dress may be only rough proxies for viewpoints. Older white males in suits do not necessarily share the same viewpoint. In that specific instance, one was from a large corporate law firm, the other an academic who had a career as a public defender. They certainly had different experiences and interests, whether or not different viewpoints.

"In Grutter[v Bollinger, 539 U.S. 306 (2003)], the Court held that the University of Michigan School of Law may consider an applicant's race in its admissions decisions, to enroll a 'critical mass of underrepresented minority students,' as a means 'in obtaining the educational benefits that flow from a diverse student body.' ...

"Some affirmative action proponents celebrated the holding as a victory. But was it really a victory for stakeholders of affirmative action programs? ...

"A closer reading of the compelling interest in terms of the prospective educational rewards derived from racial diversity at the Law School, is to examine which students actually stand to gain from this enhanced educational benefit....

"... [T]he students admitted with a plus-factor consideration of their race, are not the students for whom exposure to these same students (themselves or each other) constitute the compelling interest. The Law School's own expert for the litigation, Patricia Gurin, found that Latinos at the University of Michigan mostly come from racially diverse neighborhoods or schools, and African Americans arrive equipped with knowledge of issues surrounding race. ...

"... Students of color have such pre-exposure to racial diversity that the enhanced benefit is really not an enhanced benefit for them. The one constant in this illustration is the non-diverse (mostly white) student body. The variables are the students of color admitted under the Law School's affirmative action plan, and the enhanced educational benefit of their presence to the non-diverse student body. The compelling interest, focused on obtaining these educational benefits, is therefore mainly concerned with the non-diverse student body's diminished educational experience....

"Perhaps even more troubling than this view of the compelling interest, during the litigation of this case and the companion case, Gratz v. Bollinger, Patricia Gurin's Expert Report was used to tout the educational benefits of racial diversity. This claim is problematic when one considers that Gurin concluded that exposure to other races enhances the education of students so exposed, based on studies showing only marginal educational benefits, if any, for students of color, compared with appreciable positive correlations between racial diversity and learning and democracy outcomes for white students. Justice O'Connor's opinion in Grutter ... effectively established affirmative action for students of color to enhance the education of white students." David Kow, *The (Un)Compelling Interest for Underrepresented Minority Students: Enhancing the Education of White Students Underexposed to Racial Diversity*, 20 Berkeley La Raza L.J. 157, 161-162 (2010) (footnotes omitted).

Viewpoint Bias

The cultural lens through which we observe and discern operates most powerfully when we are unaware of its existence. When our cultural viewpoint remains hidden to us, we are unable to mediate its influence. We are unable to go beyond our own culturally influenced viewpoint to appreciate how different culture influences others differently. We remain imprisoned to some extent by our own culture when we fail to recognize how it influences our perceptions. The younger female lawyer held a cultural bias that kept her from hearing the research and commitment of an older white-male lawyer who wore a suit. She found it difficult to set aside that viewpoint long enough to hear the research that the speaker would share.

Multiple views of a subject tend to reduce viewpoint bias. Six eyewitnesses to an accident are generally better than one. Ten qualified interpreters of data are generally better than one. The reason is that the viewpoint bias of other observers mediates or cancels the viewpoint bias of one. No one viewpoint necessarily has a greater claim to truth than another viewpoint. Truth, meaning that which best represents the real or actual conditions, is a property and has a value distinct from viewpoint. Statements are no more or less true because of one's viewpoint but because they do or do not more-closely approach the reality of actual conditions.

Viewpoint Awareness

A first step toward intercultural competence as a professional then is to develop awareness of your own viewpoint. Lawyers should know the lens through which they hear clients and evaluate events and conditions. Lawyers and other professionals must be aware of their own socialization and the way that it affects their viewpoint. Developing viewpoint awareness enables you to mediate the biases of your own viewpoint. The lawyer who knows the lawyer's own viewpoint is more likely to be able to recognize how that viewpoint affects the lawyer's evaluation. The lawyer may then modify the evaluation to compensate for viewpoint bias.

Developing viewpoint awareness also enables you to value other viewpoints. The lawyer who can identify the lawyer's own viewpoint—not the lawyer's assertion but the viewpoint affecting the assertion—is more likely to be able to hear, credit, and evaluate accurately the assertion of another made from a different viewpoint. Developing viewpoint awareness also enables you to distinguish truth from your own viewpoint. Conditions may not be as your viewpoint interprets or assumes. A client may be showing respect from their viewpoint, when it looks like disrespect from your viewpoint. A client may be *unable* to do as you recommend, when it looks to you from your viewpoint that the client is instead *unwilling* to do as you recommend.

Developing viewpoint awareness also enables you to evaluate assertions independent of the person making the assertion. The young female lawyer who denigrated the older white males dressed in a suit could have, by mediating her viewpoint, listened to their assertions first and then evaluated the assertions on their truth-dependence rather than on the age, race, sex, and dress of the persons asserting them. One is never completely able to separate evaluations from one's own viewpoint or another viewpoint. The value in knowing and adjusting for one's own viewpoint is to decrease bias and increase truth awareness, meaning the ability to see situations more as they are than as one's viewpoint misrepresents them to be.

"Intrapersonal intelligence refers to the ability to distinguish and respond to our own feelings, needs, desires, and motivations, to build accurate mental models of ourselves, and to use these mental models to guide us in making important decisions about our lives. While 'emotional sensitivity' is integral to the development of intrapersonal intelligence, it is in how a person uses self-knowledge for personal and professional problem-solving that the full measure of intrapersonal intelligence is actualized.

"Lawyers do not leave their beliefs, cultural norms, and personal values at the door when they assume the roles of counselor, advisor, advocate, planner, judge or legislator. It is therefore important that we notice and monitor how our beliefs, norms, and values tend to affect our attitudes and interactions in lawyering work." Angela O. Burton, *Cultivating Ethical, Socially Responsible Lawyer Judgment: Introducing the Multiple Lawyering Intelligences Paradigm into the Clinical Setting*, 11 CLINICAL L. REV. 15, 17 (2004).

Specific Awareness

You develop awareness of your own viewpoint by first identifying it. Study the communication and relationship preferences within your own household, circle of friends, and workplace. Notice the resources that you all share. Notice how you tend to think, speak, relate, and act alike. Those similarities provide clues to your viewpoint, the perspective from which you observe events and evaluate information. You also develop awareness of your own viewpoint by discerning the viewpoints of others. Seeing how many different ways in which others can construct and interpret communication, relationships, and other conditions affecting the representation makes clearer one's own constructions. You see the color of the water in which you swim when you see that water has other colors.

When a lawyer recognizes other possible cultural constructions for communication, relationships, and other conditions affecting the representation, the lawyer is better able to understand and advise the client. The underlying model is to know yourself, know the client, and know how to respond to the knowledge that you have of the client. Study shows the value of this awareness-knowledge-skill model. Be aware of your own cultural perspectives, know alternative perspectives of others, and develop the skill to adjust for effective representation.

Inference Theory

Study also shows the value of inference theory. Inference theory encourages you to attribute client conditions to their causes rather than to presumed attributes or intentions of those clients. The proper practice is to infer causes from conditions, not from client attributes. For example, a client is not necessarily poor because they wish to be so or because they have a characteristic that makes them so. The lawyer who assumes that the client is poor because the client lacks ambition or is unmotivated and lazy, attributes the poverty to an attribute of the client rather than to possible causes of the poverty. The client may instead be poor because of a condition that caused the poverty. The condition causing the poverty may have been severe illness, serious injury, family needs, criminal conviction, lack of legal status, or other personal emergency causing job loss. The condition could also be lack of education, socialization, transportation, or job opportunity.

Identifying causes for the client's condition is a critical part of effective legal service. Inference theory, encouraging the lawyer to attribute conditions to causes rather than to attributes, especially supports effective cross-cultural service. Cross-cultural interaction hazards mistaken attribution. We more readily make incorrect attributions when we do not know the client's cultural reference. When inference theory has lawyers rely on conditions and causes rather than attributes, lawyers reduce the probability of harmful misattribution.

"Most of our townfolk were, naturally, the well-to-do, shading downward, but seldom reaching poverty. As playmate of the children I saw the homes of nearly every one, except a few immigrant New Yorkers, of whom none of us approved. The homes I saw impressed me, but did not overwhelm me. Many were bigger than mine, with newer and shinier things, but they did not seem to differ in kind. I think I probably surprised my hosts more than they me, for I was easily at home and perfectly happy and they looked to me just like ordinary people, while my brown face and frizzled hair must have seemed strange to them.

"Yet I was very much one of them. I was a center and sometimes the leader of the town gang of boys. We were noisy, but never very bad,—and, indeed, my mother's quiet influence came in here, as I realize now. She did not try to make me perfect. To her I was already perfect. She simply warned me of a few things, especially saloons. In my town the saloon was the open door to hell. The best families had their drunkards and the worst had little else.

"Very gradually,—I cannot now distinguish the steps, though here and there I remember a jump or a jolt—but very gradually I found myself assuming quite placidly that I was different from other children. At first I think I connected the difference with a manifest ability to get my lessons rather better than most and to recite with a certain happy, almost taunting, glibness, which brought frowns here and there. Then, slowly, I realized that some folks, a few, even several, actually considered my brown skin a misfortune; once or twice I became painfully aware that some human beings even thought it a crime. I was not for a moment daunted,—although, of course, there were some days of secret tears—rather I was spurred to tireless effort. If they beat me at anything, I was grimly determined to make them sweat for it! Once I remember challenging a great, hard farmer-boy to battle, when I knew he could whip me; and he did. But ever after, he was polite." W.E.B. DuBois, Darkwater—Voices from Within the Veil (Harcourt, Brace & Co. 1920) (excerpt from Chapter 1: The Shadow of Year).

Dissonance Reduction

Developing self-awareness, knowledge of others, and cross-cultural interaction skill will help you attribute a client's condition to causes rather than to the client's attributes. Our minds work constantly to create meaning out of observation, order out of chaos, even when the observations may have no meaning or pattern. We particularly try to eliminate seeming contradictions to reduce their *cognitive dissonance*, meaning the mental unease or discomfort that we feel when observations seem inconsistent. Our minds naturally resolve into patterns and explanations observations that jar or seem to conflict. The cultural lens through which we view things is one way in which we reduce dissonance and create meaning.

Without self-awareness, knowledge of others, and cross-cultural interaction skill, your cultural viewpoint might cause you to resolve contradictions and conflicts into premises and beliefs that do not reflect actual conditions. You might construe incorrectly client attributes, conditions, causes, and intentions. In making that mistake, your service may well prove ineffective. To resolve dissonance that you perceive in a client's information or circumstances, you may believe that a client has deliberately chosen a certain course, particularly when your cultural perspective would endorse that conclusion, when to the contrary other causes brought about the client's circumstance.

When you recognize your own cultural lens and the different lens through which the client views a situation, then you are less likely to attribute the client's condition to the client's different attribute or culture and more likely to attribute the client's condition to its causes. You are less likely to reduce dissonance through mistaken assumptions and more likely to resolve dissonance into a proper interpretation of cultural clues. For example, discerning whether a client intended something does not depend not on the client's attributes. Rather, intention depends on whether the client knew the behavior's consequence, desired to bring about that consequence, and believed that the client was able to do so.

The question of intention can require you to consider a range of conditions seen through the client's cultural viewpoint and circumstance. Add to the mix self-serving selectivity, cognitive dissonance reduction, and similar hazards of subjectivity (the mental practices of non-rational perceivers), and attributing a certain disposition to a client in the face of so many situational considerations can be hazardous at best and prejudicial attribution error at worst. Appreciating how viewpoint subjectivity can work together with cognitive-dissonance reduction to mislead a lawyer's judgment should make the lawyer ready to give a client the full benefit of the doubt.

General Skills

The next chapter introduces you to a framework for acquiring cross-cultural skills. Even without acquiring a framework for discerning cultural viewpoints and exercising cross-cultural skills, you can minimize the impact of your own viewpoint and avoid some attribution error by following certain practices when interacting with clients. Consider the following suggestions when serving diverse clients, to increase your cross-cultural sensitivity independent of specific cross-cultural skills:

- *Introduce yourself* in a way that puts the client at ease. Say your name. Anonymity appears aloof, insular, uncaring, and arrogant. Make eye contact unless the client studiously avoids eye contact, in which case avoid eye contact. Smile politely, while maintaining seriousness appropriate to the matter at hand. If the client appears ready to offer a handshake, then you offer a handshake first. If the client is reluctant to offer a handshake, then do not embarrass the client with an extended hand. Assume hidden rules of interaction that you do not know. Do not assume that the client should show immediate signs of appreciating your service. Law is pervasive for some clients. Some clients lack resources while having critical needs for legal help. Clients may not have any choice but to see you.

- *Expect varied communication styles,* and communicate accordingly. Not all clients share your verbal interests, styles, or skills. Clients may speak in indirect and generalized fashion, using frequent non-verbal assists. Give frequent verbal acknowledgments ("mm-hmm," "yes, I know," etc.), behavioral prompts (nodding, smiling, etc.), and emotional response (interest, sorrow, satisfaction, etc.). Indicate content uptake. Show that you actually hear and appreciate the nuances the client expresses, before responding with legal information. Do not force a client to say something the client wishes to avoid saying. Respect the circular nature of some communication preferences. Avoid power struggles over language. Use calm, non-judgmental, adult voice. Never command or scold in parent voice. Never use defensive or emotional child voice. Acknowledge and appreciate the client's humor. Use metaphor and story as a guide. Draw diagrams. Recognize cultural references, accepting and employing them to contextualize and communicate solutions.

- **Ask why the client is seeing you** before making any assumptions. Ask open-ended questions like, "What worries you?" "How may I help?" or "What do you want to happen?" Respect the client's freedom and personality. Do not assume that the client has purely legal goals. Legal goals may be enmeshed in social, political, moral, financial, familial, ethical, personal, and spiritual goals, or legal goals may be absent. Assist with more than purely legal goals where your life experience enables you. Refer the client for other help with non-legal goals. Legal solutions are not the only solutions. Think in terms of broad, team solutions. Help the client avoid unproductive negative thoughts and influences.

- **Listen to the client's judgment** rather than to your own judgment about what is important. Let the client decide. Do not dismiss the client's hopes, goals, expectations, and objectives, even when you would choose different objectives. Consider the client's goals even when they appear to you to be unachievable. The client's active pursuit of an unrealistic but safe goal can serve the client by indirectly achieving more useful objectives. Clients can learn useful skills and develop helpful practices and habits when pursuing even unachievable goals. Listen for words that seem out of place to you. They may be clues to a resource, habit, or understanding on which the client can draw for solutions. Develop context for the client's situation, whether personal, medical, legal, family, or social context. Develop factual content where you see a legal issue that you can help address. Clients may express emotions and opinions leaving it to you to prompt for relevant facts.

- **Watch the client** with an eye sensitive to the client's reactions. Summarize the client's goals and your advice on how to achieve them. If the client does not share your confidence in the solution you proposed, then you may not have understood the client properly, or you may have assumed that the client has capabilities and resources that the client does not have. Continue to listen, ask, summarize, suggest, and generate other options until the client appears satisfied with your advice. What seems to you to be readily achievable may in fact not be for reasons only the client can appreciate. Suggest and teach coping strategies. Gently let the client know that you are offering bridges out of negative situations.

- **Explain steps** to the client in manageable components. Think of each step that a larger task requires, and then explain those steps for the client. Clients may lack the ability to break down larger tasks into manageable components. Help the client do so. When the steps become too many, stop, return to the first step that the client can understand and follow, and then plan another consultation for the rest of the steps. Watch for signs that the client is overwhelmed or frustrated. Assign to the client only those tasks that the client believes are clearly manageable. Model self-talking through procedures. Propose role models. Clients can benefit more through mentors and relationships than through systems and actions. Be a coach, not a commander, judge, or task-master. Speak about choices and consequences. Help the client identify cause and effect (impulse and consequence) relationships.

- **Confirm the plan** that you have developed. Ask the client if the client would like you to write down the plan. If you do write it down, then do so in clearly legible handwriting and with numbered steps. Clients may lack the planning and initiating skills that you possess. Help them prioritize and plan. Then help them record the plan in a manner that they can understand and use. Then help them confirm that the plan will lead them toward their objective. Ensure throughout that they believe that they have the resources available to follow the plan. Do not plan anything for which the client lacks the resources. Solutions are not systems. They are relationships leading to small steps in the right direction. Distinguish your responsibility from the client's responsibility. Be responsible *to* the client for the steps that you say that you will perform. Make it clear to them what you are and are not going to do for them.

- ***Express hope and optimism*** about the client's situation no matter how dire it may seem to you. Building and maintaining hope is essential for clients who have few resources or large challenges. You may have a client whose legal situation cannot be addressed. Yet through your discussion of it and your continuing relationship with the client, the client may develop other achievable objectives. Be frank in your advice, but do not destroy the client's confidence with overly harsh advice. Stress the client's internal assets—perhaps the client's perseverance, discernment, ethics, or faith.

- ***Listen for a parting request*** from the client. The consultation does not end until the client has left. Just because you think it is over, does not mean that it is over. Some clients will use the consultation time simply to develop trust and understanding and only introduce the important matter when you think the consultation is over. It is not always about what you think it is about. Be prepared to pick up on a small parting comment and to address new legal issues at what you thought was the conclusion of the session. Be sure to elicit any lingering concerns with a question like, "Is there anything else about which we should talk?"

- ***Tell the client when you are next available*** for further consultation, especially if time did not permit you to answer all of the client's questions and address all of the client's legal issues. To some clients, the relationship with you is more important than the service you provide. Some clients benefit not through service but through relationship. Letting the client know that you value the relationship may contribute more to the client's situation than any legal service you are able to provide. If you cannot be a mentor, then think of and offer one.

"[C]ognitive errors and shortcuts form formidable barrier to the advancement of under-represented women [] and also non-immigrant[], primarily indigenous groups (that is, American Indians, Mexican Americans, Puerto Rican Americans, Native Hawaiians, and African Americans. The fifteen errors include: first impressions, elitism, longing to clone, shifting standards and raising the bar, pre-mature ranking, psychoanalyzing job candidates and others, and *above all* negative and positive stereotypes (biases) related to gender and to group membership. In my consulting work, I now use this cognitive-errors approach to help academics develop recognition of typical errors and then rise above them." MOODY, JOANN, FACULTY DIVERSITY—REMOVING THE BARRIERS (Routledge 2012).

Reflections

Consider the following reflections on viewpoint subjectivity. Add these reflections to your journal. Find an acquaintance with whom to discuss these questions, or organize a group discussion, to broaden and enrich your view:

1. What is the earliest event that you can recall in your life? Does it provide any clue to your disposition, worldview, or viewpoint?

2. Identify the five most significant events in your life. How do they each reflect, influence, construct, or affect your worldview or viewpoint? Which of these five events would you expect that others share, having experienced similar events? Which of them would you expect that others do not share, not having experienced similar events?

3. Identify an event in your life that you wish others could share for the inspiration, insight, or other benefits it gave you. Now, identify an event that you wish you could experience that you think would give you the greatest inspiration, insight, or other benefits.

4. Can you think of a specific person who experienced an event that you wish you could experience for the inspiration, insight, or other benefits it would give you?

5. If you could interview anyone currently living, then who would it be, and why would you choose them? How do you think the interview might affect how you view future events?

6. If you could interview anyone who lived in the past, then who would it be, and why would you choose them? How do you think the interview might affect how you view future events?

7. Can you give an example of when a change in the economy, national security, energy prices, credit or finance, the cost or availability of education, employment rates, the availability of medical care, or other broad factors affected you personally? What resources do you have (personal, familial, social, educational, financial, political, etc.) to mitigate the effect of outside factors on your life?

8. How effective are you at discerning probable causes or contributing factors to significant events that occur in your life? Can you think of an example when you could see causes or contributing factors in the lives of clients or others that they could not discern for themselves?

Chapter 6

Structural

"What did *I* ever do that was wrong!"

Character

The cross-cultural client came into the soup kitchen's conference room on crutches. The lawyer helped him close the door and ease into a chair. "Not easy getting around the street on crutches," the client said as he smiled at the lawyer, not as a complaint but an apology acknowledging the lawyer's help with the door and chair.

"So, what's going on?" the lawyer asked, adding, "My guess is that you're not usually laid up this way." The lawyer could tell from the client's strong handshake, rough hands, lean frame, and work clothes that the client might ordinarily have been quite able to ambulate.

"You guessed right, lawyer," the client chuckled back. The client then explained that for years he had lived down the street at the hotel, riding the bus back and forth across town to hold down two jobs. He lived frugally, sending all of his money other than the little that spent on his own meager existence to his daughter who had two children and needed his support. "I guess I should have kept a little for myself for a rainy day," the client concluded, "Because now I'm nearly out on the street."

The client explained that he had been crossing the street at a crosswalk and light when a vehicle ran into him. The collision had not broken bones but had torn ligaments in his knee and caused a severe ankle sprain that remained badly swollen. The client had not worked since, for months. "Without insurance, they won't take me at the clinic for my therapy," the client said, "when I need it to get better and get back to work."

The lawyer explained the client's no-fault insurance rights to collect work-loss benefits and obtain reimbursement for 100% of his medical expense. "I know all about that," the client replied, "But the insurance company doesn't believe me. They think I'm faking it, but look at me. What did I ever do here that was wrong?"

The client's last statement pained the lawyer who knew the suspicion with which some insurance claim representatives regarded some claimants, particularly those who lived at society's margins. This client, though, had certainly done nothing wrong. He had somehow even managed on his own to get a copy of the police official accident report, ambulance report, and emergency-room visit to the insurer, which also had his authorization for release of medical and employment information.

Within a couple of weeks, after a demand letter and couple of telephone calls to the insurer, the lawyer had helped the client get the work-loss benefits to pay his weekly hotel rent and the reimbursement to complete his physical therapy. The lawyer knew that sometimes all it takes is vouching for a client's character, which the lawyer had quite deliberately done in his detailed demand letter to the insurer and calls with its claim representative.

"You're looking a lot better," the lawyer greeted the client in the soup kitchen's conference room another month later, "Did you get frustrated and break up those crutches?" The client had only a slight limp, the lawyer noticed as he offered him a chair. The client laughed at the lawyer's joke and shook his head, declining the chair offer.

"I'm back at work, both jobs," the client said with a huge smile, extending his hand to the lawyer for a warm handshake that turned into an embarrassed hug. "Just wanted to thank you," the client added in a choked voice, his eyes glistening. He then walked quickly out, a strong and simple man of sterling character devoted to providing for himself, his daughter, and his grandchildren.

Judging by Character

Martin Luther King Jr.'s famous 1963 Washington Mall Dream Speech included the unforgettable line, "I have a dream that my four little children will one day live in a nation where they will not be judged by the color of their skin but by the content of their character." To be judged by the content of one's character rather than the color of one's skin has rich ethical meaning, particularly for lawyers. It first admonishes us, in our legal service to clients, to avoid bias and prejudice particularly based on ethnicity or race but likely also on culture and class. The above chapters have illustrated forms and cognitive sources of bias and prejudice.

Yet Dr. King's dream speech also encourages us to look more deeply into the content of our clients' character. He offered both a *proscription* not to judge by skin color and a *prescription* to instead judge by character. He may have meant to suggest that to accomplish one (not judge by skin color), one must do the other (judge by character). Judging, evaluation, or discernment may at least to some degree be necessary particularly in professional relationships where clients expect advice and action. Many have given substantial attention to the proscription not to judge by skin color, just as this book has done in the above five chapters. Yet fewer attend to the prescription to judge instead by character, which may be appropriate, necessary, or inevitable.

In the broader sense, within the rich content of our remarkably various characters influenced by our inevitably unique individual experiences, we are all multicultural, no one of us more than another, but each drawing habits, disciplines, practices, styles, and preferences from here and there over the course of our lives to create our own unique perspectives. If character is indeed that varied, and judging by external attributes like skin color is that hazardous, then lawyers should base client relationship on discernment of each client's unique character.

"Efforts during the past ten years to diversify America's law schools by enrolling more African-American students have failed because those responsible for law school admissions and accreditation practices have created a de facto and racially discriminatory quota system that restricts African-American access to the legal profession.

"African-Americans comprise approximately 13% of the United States population. The total number of African-Americans enrolled at all ABA-approved law schools peaked in 1994 at 9681 students, which at that time represented 7.5% of all enrolled students. Total law school enrollment in 1994 was 128,989 students, and total minority enrollment was 24,611 students.

"From 1994-2004, total law school enrollment increased to 140,376 students (+8.8%) and total minority enrollment increased to 29,489 students (+19.8%). But, total African-American enrollment decreased from 9681 to 9488 students (-2%), which represents just 6.8% of all enrolled students.

"This same pattern repeats itself in the total number of J.D. degrees awarded to African-American graduates of ABA-approved law schools. This number peaked in 1998 at 2943 degrees awarded. Since then, while the total number of degrees awarded to all law school graduates increased to 40,018 in 2004 (+1.4%), the total number of degrees awarded to African-American graduates during the same period decreased to 2719 (-7.6%).

"These statistics make clear that American legal education is moving backwards, not forwards, in providing access to law school for African-American students. Simultaneously, the number and percentage of African-American students enrolled in ABA-approved schools and of African-American graduates of those schools decreased while the number and percentage of African-American applicants in the pipeline to law school also decreased." John Nussbaumer, *Misuse of the Law School Admissions Test, Racial Discrimination, and the De Facto Quota System for Restricting African-American Access to the Legal Profession*, 80 St. John's L.Rev. 167 (2006) (footnote omitted).

Access to Justice

What did Dr. King mean specifically by "judged ... by the content of their character"? He was certainly addressing equal opportunity for education, employment, housing, and other rights and privileges. He was promoting access to social opportunity. To lawyers, the concept of *access* implies access *to justice* through legal services. A lawyer's legal service is not to educate, employ, or house, at least directly. A lawyer's legal service is to provide access to justice. Justice may result in education, employment, or housing. Yet the admonition to provide access means for lawyers to provide legal service in ways that help clients reach justice.

To a lawyer, the admonition to judge by character implies finding sound bases within the client's character on which to promote legal services that provide access to justice. Lawyers necessarily or inevitably make judgments about clients. Lawyers must direct those judgments toward character, not skin color, in ways that help lawyers better communicate with, understand, and serve clients in a professional and ethical manner.

Professional Socialization

Law schools reasonably expect law students to learn and be able to adopt in certain settings the professional culture of lawyers. Bar associations have the same expectations of lawyers. Common professional culture promotes the commitments and interactive practices of lawyers. Clients draw benefits from lawyers being able to share a single professional culture. On the other hand, law schools and bar associations need not expect law students and lawyers to assimilate to the degree that they adopt professional culture in all settings. Professional training and practice does not require relinquishing personal affinities for and skills with other cultures. Professional practice may instead benefit when a lawyer preserves the skills to interact with other cultures.

Lawyers can alternate cultures. Within the confines of conduct rules, lawyers can use professional culture in court and other settings where professional culture is a resource and reasonable expectation, while adopting other cultural practices in other settings where those other practices would be a greater resource and a reasonable expectation. Lawyers should ensure that their own professional training and socialization does not inhibit them from drawing on broader cultural skills. Lawyers should develop and retain the ability to recognize and respond appropriately to the variety of interests, resources, and practices of diverse clients.

"Lawyers and clients who do not share the same culture face special challenges in developing a trusting relationship in which genuine and accurate communication can occur. ...

"Even in situations in which trust is established, students may experience cultural differences that significantly interfere with lawyers' and clients' capacities to understand one another's goals, behaviors and communications. Cultural differences often cause us to attribute different meaning to the same set of facts. One important goal of cross-cultural training is to help students make isomorphic attributions, i.e., to attribute to behavior and communication that which is intended by the actor or speaker. Students who are taught about the potential for misattribution can develop strategies for checking themselves and their interpretations.

"Inaccurate attributions can cause lawyers to make significant errors in their representation of clients. Imagine a lawyer saying to a client, 'If there is anything that you do not understand, please just ask me to explain' or 'If I am not being clear, please just ask me any questions.' The lawyer might assume that a client who does not then ask for clarification surely understands what the lawyer is saying. However, many cultural differences may explain a client's reluctance to either blame the lawyer for poor communication (the second question) or blame himself or herself for lack of understanding (the first question). Indeed, clients from some cultures might find one or the other of these results to be rude and, therefore, will feel reluctant to ask for clarification for fear of offending the lawyer or embarrassing himself." Susan Bryant, *The Five Habits: Building Cross-Cultural Competence in Lawyers*, 8 CLIN. L. REV. 33, 42-43 (2001) (footnotes omitted).

Frameworks or Heuristics

Law schools and bar associations increasingly help lawyers develop, retain, and exercise cross-cultural skills. They do so through various articulated or unarticulated frameworks. Discerning how culture constructs the different viewpoints of diverse clients is difficult without an interpretive framework or heuristic. A *framework* or *heuristic* is a cognitive construction that guides thinking and action. Heuristics can be either explicit or implicit. You can be aware of the framework or unaware of it, employing it consciously or subconsciously.

Lawyers use heuristics or frameworks to develop strategies and exercise skills in many areas. Lawyers conduct intake sessions, evaluate claims, prioritize tasks, and select procedures through heuristics either learned explicitly or, more often, intuited and adopted through experience. You can use a heuristic to learn and employ effective cross-cultural service. This chapter introduces a framework for discerning the cultural viewpoints or lenses through which diverse clients may operate. The next several chapters articulate the framework into something useful for you in your law practice.

Heuristic Criteria

Consider some criteria by which you should judge this framework or any others that you may learn. These criteria may help give you confidence that the framework is meaningful. A useful framework for a lawyer to judge a diverse client's cultural viewpoint or character would be one that is first of all clear. You should be able to comprehend the framework. The framework should also cohere, that is, form a unity. It should describe client characteristics, while it should also prescribe how to respond to those characteristics.

A useful framework should also be unique, outside of what lawyers already know and share. The framework should also be valid, meaning that it should accomplish what the lawyer sets out to accomplish in improving cross-cultural skills. The framework should be essential. Unless the lawyer's services approximate the skills for which the framework calls, those services should be cross-culturally ineffectual. The framework should also be of a simple design while capable of supporting the complex. Simplicity aids recall and use. You would be unlikely to able to recall and use a complex framework. Yet the framework should be able to help you discern the relatively complex combination of characteristics with which clients present.

Overall, the framework should encourage a sort of interactive professional *multi-dimensionality*. You can learn to see yourself as more than one dimensional or mono-cultural. You do so through positive internal dialogue guiding how you construct your observations of clients and shaping your behaviors toward them. Individuals are in some respects like all others, like some others, and like no others. Lawyers see clients at three levels: the universal, the group, and the individual. We need the skills to better see and understand how these levels work together to form the unique dignity of each client—to make, in the social-psychology lexicon introduce in above chapters, better *idiographic assessment*.

"One barrier is what most white people were taught to believe about how to be fair to black people—justice equals color-blindness. I have my doubts about whether people can actually be color blind, but maybe it is possible. I don't want to argue that point. I do know that it is absolutely true that many white people are blind to the impact of color. If my friends remain color-blind, I will forever be the only black person at the party, and they will have no appreciation for the impact that this repeated experience has on me. Being the only black person at a social event is not the biggest deal in the world, and I don't want my white friends to stop inviting me to their events! After all, when it comes to a party, I am free to accept the invitation or not, to come and go as I please.

"However, if you think about how this type of underrepresentation plays out at work, in the classroom, on a committee day after day, you can imagine the isolation that many black people feel and how it affects their sense of belonging." Verna Myers, *Moving Diversity Forward—How to Go from Well-Meaning to Well-Doing* 27 (ABA 2011).

A Five-Dimension Framework

The framework that the rest of this book employs involves five *dimensions* that lawyers experience with every client. Your sensitive treatment of those five dimensions should place you on a solid cross-cultural foundation with any client. The five dimensions involve considering the client's (1) communication, (2) cognition, (3) reference, (4) resources, and (5) relationship. Put another way, the five dimensions are (1) linguistic, (2) logical, (3) narrative, (4) strategic, and (5) personal.

Lawyers should possess intercultural competence in at least these five dimensions because every client speaks, thinks, refers to shared knowledge, strategizes from resources, and relates. These five dimensions linguistic, logical, narrative, strategic, and personal articulate *multiple intelligences* through which clients operate. Improved cross-cultural skill in one dimension works synergistically to improve skill in other dimensions. Your sensitive idiographic assessment of these five dimensions should improve your skill in cross-cultural service. Consider the following outline of each dimension.

Communication

Communication sensitivity comes first because of the significance of how we speak and listen. Communication varies. The communication that one client understands and appreciates another client may take as offense. Lawyers should above all be sensitive listeners and speakers in client interaction.

You must first appreciate the form or *register* in which your client wishes and expects to communicate. For some lawyers, the thought that clients speak in different registers is itself new. Law school and practice acculturate lawyers to speak in a single shared register. Lawyers sometimes fail to recognize other registers in which clients commonly speak. Effective lawyers intuitively employ a range of registers depending on the client's register preference. Effective lawyers adjust to client register, not the other way around. Lawyers adapt to meet client register because register connects closely to client emotional state, cognitive practice, and relationship preference. The following chapter explains communication registers in detail.

> "All lawyers must strive to understand their client, communicate clearly and effectively, and help their client succeed in the legal system. Pro bono lawyers representing people in chronic poverty often will find that the concrete steps to achieving these goals play out in unfamiliar ways. Pro bono clients have grown up in a different world with different survival skills. In order for the legal system to work effectively for these clients, pro bono lawyers need sensitivity, awareness, and extra diligence. Successfully understanding and accommodating these differences results in higher quality services to the client and a greater level of satisfaction for the attorney for a job well-done." Martha Delaney, *Working Effectively with Pro Bono Clients*, 62-Aug. Bench & B. Minn. 24, 26 (2005).

Cognition

Like communication, client cognitive practices also vary. Lawyers learn certain cognitive practices. They learn to think alike, in the manner that lawyers think to solve problems. The manner in which lawyers think is a powerful professional tool. Clients though do not always think like lawyers. Clients seldom think with the purpose, order, and clarity of lawyers. Clients think in ways that make sense in the cultures in which they operate. Yet many clients seldom if ever operate within professional culture like the culture of lawyers, meaning that those clients may seldom if ever think like lawyers.

Lawyers need to be sensitive to the manner in which clients think. Lawyers need to recognize how clients are thinking, especially when those clients are thinking unlike lawyers. Effective lawyers adjust their legal advice and service to account for the different thinking of clients. Lawyers adjust to client thinking, not the other way around, client adjusting to lawyer. Lawyers find ways to deliver their advice to account for how the client will process that advice. A later chapter explains differences in cognitive practices and how to recognize and remediate them.

Resources

Like communication and cognition, client resources also vary. Lawyers generally have like resources including education, licensure, communication means, finances, offices, transportation, professional networks, and control of schedule. The resources of a lawyer are abundant and powerful. Lawyers may not immediately realize it, but one of their significant professional services is that they employ and deploy abundant capital on their clients' behalf, including tangible resources like offices and transportation, and financial resources like the advance of expenses, but also intangible resources like networks and reputation. Resources help to define the norms and expectations within which lawyers operate.

Clients do not always share the resources of lawyers. Clients may have different resources. Client resources may be greater than lawyer resources, are often less than lawyer resources, but are most frequently simply different from lawyer resources. For example, a client may have more or less education, money, time, liberty, standing, mobility, stability, and control over schedule than the lawyer whom the client retains. Even more significantly for some matters, a client may lack a legal status and rights and privileges that accompany that status. A client's status, record, reputation, network, social support, mental or physical health, and other resources will often differ markedly from the lawyer's resources.

Lawyers need to be sensitive to the different resources that clients have. You should not simply assume that every client has your resources or that every client has the same resources. Assuming the same resources can show insensitivity to important socioeconomic limitations and other resource differences. Lawyers need to recognize how differences in resources can affect a client's ability to follow and benefit from a lawyer's advice. Effective lawyers adjust their legal advice and service to account for different client resources. A later chapter explains in detail how client resources differ and affect a lawyer's advice.

References

Like communication, cognition, and resources, client reference systems also vary. Lawyers share certain cultural references. Professional education and practice bring to lawyers a wealth of shared information from like sources. Those shared sources include cases, commentary, professional journals, and other media. Shared sources create common history, commitments, and meaning that become communication markers and trust points among lawyers. Lawyers' cultural references are clear and powerful, creating for lawyers a view of how social relationships operate. A lawyer's professional reference system helps to define the norms and expectations within which lawyers work with and in opposition to one another. Lawyers can use with one another a single word, phrase, or similar short reference to communicate a set of expectations.

"Discrimination is behavior. It is the action we take in reference to an individual once an explicit or implicit bias has morphed from an image in our

91

heads to an exaggerated belief about a group to a judgment about that group. In other words, most of our biases are latent until a situation causes us to use our biases instead of direct knowledge to make decisions. We discriminate using both positive and negative biases, and we tend to discriminate in favor of people who are in our in-group and against those who are in our out-groups." ARIN N. REEVES, THE NEXT IQ: THE NEXT LEVEL OF INTELLIGENCE FOR 21ST CENTURY LEADERS 116-117 (American Bar Association 2012).

Clients do not always share the cultural reference system of lawyers. Clients may have different reference systems. Client reference systems may be more or less highly developed than lawyer reference systems, more or less historical, and more or less literate, but are often simply different from a lawyer's professional reference system. For example, a client may embrace a different national history, vocational experience, sports-team or sports-league commitment, sacred text, literary genre, philosophical viewpoint, psychological presentation, or social construction than the lawyer whom the client retains. Those differences may cause the client to view events and expectations differently from the lawyer.

Lawyers need to be sensitive to the different cultural references that clients have. You should not simply assume that every client has your set of cultural references and viewpoints or that every client has the same viewpoint. Assuming the same cultural references can show insensitivity to important cultural differences. Lawyers need to recognize how differences in cultural references and viewpoint can affect a client's ability and willingness to follow and benefit from a lawyer's advice. Effective lawyers adjust their legal advice and service to account for different client reference systems. A later chapter explains in detail how client references differ and affect a lawyer's advice.

Relationships

Like communication, cognition, resources, and references, client relationship preferences also vary. Lawyers share certain ways of relating. Professional practice encourages lawyers to construct their relationships with clients and others in transactional patterns. Lawyers naturally and wisely commoditize their services, affecting how lawyers relate to clients. Commoditized services affect not only how lawyers relate to clients but also how lawyers expect clients to relate to them. These transactional relationship patterns are powerful influences. Pushing transactional relationship to its limit, everything becomes an exchange. Within professional culture, even clients can begin to look like commodities. The way that lawyers relate defines norms and expectations within which lawyers work with and for clients.

Lawyers may expect clients to share their relationship preferences, but clients often do not understand, appreciate, or wish to adopt certain professional-relationship preferences. Clients may have different relationship preferences from lawyers. Clients may value the lawyer's relationship more or less than the transaction that the lawyer offers. Clients may wish to construct and maintain the relationship in a different pattern than the lawyer's usual transactional relationship. For example, a client may wish to have a more interdependent than independent relationship with the lawyer, one in which the lawyer has more authority to act for the client. The client may alternatively desire advice that accounts for the client's interests within the client's family or community rather than solely or primarily as an individual. Differences in the way that a client views and prefers relationship may cause the client to evaluate options differently from the lawyer.

Lawyers need to be sensitive to the different relationship preferences that clients have. You should not simply assume that every client has your relationship preferences or that every client has the same preference even if different from your own preference. Assuming the same relationship preferences can show insensitivity to important client differences. Lawyers need to recognize how differences in client relationship preferences can affect a client's willingness to appreciate and benefit from a lawyer's advice. Effective lawyers adjust their legal advice and service to account for different client relationship preferences. A later chapter explains in detail how client relationship preferences differ and affect a lawyer's advice.

> "[N]on-judgmental thinking is required to develop connection to and understanding of clients. A cross-cultural anthropologist has referred to this as the capacity to enter the cultural imagination of another, or as "perceiving as normal things that at first seem bizarre or strange." Remaining non-judgmental is a core cross-cultural skill and one that is particularly difficult for lawyers. Our training includes being called upon in classroom discussion to judge a case based on limited, digested casebook facts. Early in most representations, lawyers begin to assess clients' stories and the likely result in the case. Students are often taught that assessing client credibility is a critical piece of the lawyers' role that begins in the initial interview. Although assessing the viability of a case is an important lawyering skill, cultural differences or incorrect assumptions of similarity may lead to ethnocentric distortion of the lawyer's assessments." Susan Bryant, *The Five Habits: Building Cross-Cultural Competence in Lawyers*, 8 Clin. L. Rev. 33, 41 (2001) (footnotes omitted).

Developing the Framework

The rest of this book explores the above framework and specific skills for competence in cross-cultural service. To escape the prison of cultural bias, recognize the silent language that takes you and your client beyond culture and, with it, beyond bias. Make the effort to interact in service and subordinate relationships with unlike others. Increase your contact with members of other cultures, races, socioeconomic classes, religions, and groups unlike those to which you belong. Appreciate too that if you are serving a client who exercises different habits than your own, you have already demonstrated the first intercultural competence, which is openness to the miracle of individual identity, experience, and variety.

Reflections

Consider the following reflections on diversity frameworks. Add these reflections to your journal. Find an acquaintance with whom to discuss these questions, or organize a group discussion, to broaden and enrich your view:

1. Surely, you have recognized that people vary in the way that they communicate. Have you ever thought deliberately about the differences you hear in communication styles? Do you have any framework for evaluating the form of communication? Have

you had any education in communication? If so, then how does that education inform you about how different people communicate differently? Is it sufficient to adjust your communication intuitively, or do you see a value to communication studies? How important is communication to lawyers? What would improve your intuitive communication skills with diverse clients, if not explicit study?

2. Do you think that people vary in the way that they think about legal problems? Have you ever studied how lay persons like clients might deliberate over legal problems differently? How do you think that your thinking about a legal problem differs from a client's thinking? Do you feel that you should account for the client's different thinking when advising the client? Or is it sufficient to address a client as you would address a lawyer who had a legal problem on which you were advising?

3. When was the last time that you noticed a client or other person make a reference to something unfamiliar to you? Did you explore the reference? Do you think that it might have given you a clue to the client's thinking? Do you recognize that your own worldview may be distinct from the worldview or perspective of others including at least some of your clients? How might your worldview be distinct? What different worldviews do you think you might encounter? Have you ever studied alternative worldviews? How important is a client's worldview to a lawyer? Should the client's worldview make any difference to the advice that a lawyer gives on the client's matter?

4. Do you think that you generally have greater resources than the clients whom you serve? Do your clients' resources differ from one another? Think of an example of a client who had significantly greater or lesser resources than another client. Did it make any difference to your evaluation of the client's matter and advice you gave? Do you have any clients who have greater resources than you have? How are your resources different from the resources of most of your clients?

5. How do you treat clients differently from family members? How do you treat clients differently from opposing counsel and

parties? How do you treat clients differently from friends and other non-client acquaintances? How do you treat them alike? Would you greet a client whom you met by chance in public on the sidewalk? Would you treat them any differently under that circumstance than if they visited you in the office for advice on their matter?

Chapter 7

Communicative

"Quit fancying up his words!"

Communication Reflecting Bias

So much more than what meets the ear lies implicit in communication. Consider the following example.

The lawyer spoke only English. The client, a shy Guatemalan woman whose first language was a little-known Central American dialect, spoke just enough Spanish to communicate with the Mexican-American translator who spoke English as a second language. The lawyer discerned from the Guatemalan client's hesitancy and tearfulness that she was having difficulty speaking about her legal problem at all, no less translating it into Spanish for the Mexican-American translator to translate into English. The lawyer adjusted his own English advice accordingly, speaking more like a parent or close friend than a lawyer, even though he had never met the client.

The novice Mexican-American translator had not recognized the lawyer's shift in registers or, if she had recognized it, was unwilling to accommodate the shy Guatemalan client. The lawyer could tell from the client's increasing anxiety, tearfulness, and confusion that a communication problem was developing. As the communication problem grew more and more acute, an observing translator-trainer took over from the novice translator. Immediately, the shy client brightened, warming to the trainer's communication. Quickly understanding and trusting the trainer, the shy Guatemalan client opened her large bag and drew papers from it for the lawyer to review.

By the end of the consultation, the lawyer had confirmed for the client that everything about her matter was in order and that she need only wait for the anticipated notice of approval. The client was no longer anxiously tearful. She left relieved and grateful, having found the reassurance that she had hoped to achieve when seeking the consultation. As soon as the client left, the trainer turned to the novice translator, berating her for dressing up the lawyer's intentionally plain-spoken words into what had apparently sounded to the client like high-minded condemnation. The client's emotional condition had kept her from processing the mistranslated communication. "You must learn to translate *the register*," the trainer scolded the novice translator, adding, "Didn't you see that the lawyer was trying to reassure her?"

After the novice translator left, the trainer explained to the lawyer that the educated Mexican-American translator probably looked down on the poor Guatemalan. "She was lording it over her, you know what I mean?" asked the trainer, explaining cross-cultural relationship problems and tendencies that the trainer had observed among various Central-American populations with conflict history and different socioeconomic class, education, and resources.

Communication Framework

Competence in cross-cultural communication does not mean being able to work with translators. The above incident simply shows how a sensitive awareness and use of *language register* can mediate implicit bias, when roles and expectations interfere with sensitive communication. Language is experiential. Our use of it reflects what we have acquired through experience. Behind the words lie beliefs, attitudes, dispositions, meanings, and commitments built on those experiences.

Just as lawyers use words and phrases that convey inside meanings understood among lawyers, the specific and sometimes odd words that *clients* use can clue lawyers to *client* experiences, like similar *linguistic signposts*. The attentive lawyer attuned to intercultural communication treats words as clues, even as *links*, not only to the unique experience of the client but to the way that the client thinks and relates. Culture is a silent language. Communication reveals that silent language to those professionals capable of hearing and interpreting it. As the above example suggests, a communication framework can help generate tools, methods, and insights for lawyers to better understand and serve clients in cross-cultural representation.

"Perhaps your law firm regularly does international business or maybe you're just dipping your toe into international waters with a new client. Regardless, understanding the local business practices and cultural norms of a foreign land can help you build lasting relationships with your clients and put you ahead of the competition.

"At the American Bar Association Annual Meeting in Chicago, a panel of experts met to discuss this topic and share their personal experiences. 'Negotiating Agreements in a Cross Cultural Setting—When No Means Yes,' was sponsored by the Section of Real Property, Trust and Estate and drew from the expertise of lawyers and international business leaders.

"Panelist Arnettia Wright of the Wright Law Group presented an overview of common business and cultural practices in the Arab world. From adopting a passive and patient role, to understanding that in the Arab world, 'yes' can mean 'perhaps,' Wright stressed that doing business there requires flexibility. Wright encouraged participants to build an extra day into their trips in expectation of rescheduled or delayed meetings, which is normal.

"Doing business with China likewise can present unexpected challenges that require confidence, patience and understanding, said panelist Jia Zhao of the firm of Baker and McKenzie's Chicago office. Zhao noted that many of the legal roadblocks or business setbacks often stem from the extreme length of the negotiation process in China. Citing China's bureaucracy, politics and history, Zhao noted that the culture of business dealings there has been shaped by the restrictions imposed by the socialist system.

"Byron Buck, a lawyer for Caterpillar Investment Company, shared a personal story involving the language barrier in China. Land excavating machines are translated as 'shovels,' so Buck thought that his business partners where talking about smaller garden tools rather than huge land moving equipment." *When "Yes" Means "No"—Negotiating in Cross-Cultural Settings* (ABA Aug. 1, 2009).

Language Registers

As the above example also illustrates, the communication framework this chapter offers is that of *language register*. A *register* is an integrated set of language conventions built around the speaker's mental, emotional, and relationship expectations.

Clients of diverse backgrounds may speak in different language registers than those that you typically employ in professional settings. Professional communication has its own language register, which is often distinct from the register that clients habitually employ. Professionals can learn to change registers quickly and easily as they communicate with different persons in different settings. Be sensitive to register, or you may fail to understand, serve, and support diverse clients. Your ability to comprehend the client's situation and condition, relate to the client effectively, and appreciate the client's goals and interests, can depend on your comprehension and skillful use of language register.

Language has a multitude of different registers. This chapter offers as examples five registers that educator Ruby Payne identifies in writings that, while insightful in respects and appreciated by many, scholars rightly critique in other respects. The authors join in that critique while acknowledging the value of communication frameworks and studies stimulated by educator Payne's work. Also, linguistics experts might identify other registers than those here employed. The significance for your work as a lawyer is not memorizing specific registers but recognizing that they differ and that their differences can represent significant clues to a client's family history, culture, personal commitments, emotional condition, relationship preferences, and other factors.

The five registers discussed below are in a hierarchy from least formal to most formal. The hierarchy from least formal to most formal is to help you remember the registers. The hierarchy also indicates that your best practice is usually to match the client's register or to be within one register away from the client's register, within this hierarchy. If you speak in a register two or more registers away from the client's register, then you may offend or confuse the client.

One caution: do not let language registers tempt you into a new set of biases. Clients of all socioeconomic classes and cultures may employ each of these language registers in different settings and at different times. Avoid allowing biases and stereotypes to influence your choice of register or the response you make to the register that a client uses.

Intimate Register

Intimate register assumes complete and implicit trust between speaker and listener. Intimate register blurs the line of independence and individual responsibility into something closer to responsible superior/dependent subordinate relationship or one of mutual dependence. Intimate register does not imply physical intimacy but rather emotional closeness approximating mental intimacy. Culture, age, sex, education, socioeconomic status, mental or emotional condition, specific events, and other factors can influence whether an individual will use intimate register in certain settings. An individual's emotional condition may cause the individual to lapse into and out of intimate register.

Individuals often employ intimate register in family relationships, although not in every family, and not between all family members. Some families reserve intimate register for spouses, parents and children, siblings, or other pairings within the family. For example, in some families, only the father or mother might use intimate register only with one another or only with certain children. Some families and some family members do not use intimate register. Individuals may also employ or attempt to employ intimate register in dependent relationships when wishing to treat roles with implicit trust, as within family relationships.

Clients of lawyers may use intimate register in professional consultations, although obviously for reasons somewhat different than those relating to its use in family and social settings. Clients occasionally employ intimate register in cries for help or other emotion-based, personal interaction at less than arms-length.

Examples can include pleading ("You must help me. I have no one else to whom to turn."), weeping ("How could you do that to me, deny me when I most need your help?"), or expressing anger or frustration when given ambiguous advice rather than direction ("Just tell me what to do, and I will do it."). The client depicted at the beginning of this chapter gives an example of a client speaking through a translator in an intimate, child-like manner, probably hoping and expecting that the lawyer would reciprocate by communicating in the manner of a concerned parent.

A client's use of intimate register in professional consultations may indicate unfamiliarity with other language registers. In some household, peer, and work environments, intimate register is the only or primary register. Clients who have little experience outside of those environments and lack exposure to other registers may be unfamiliar with and confused by them. Those clients may also take the use of other registers as a rejection of their habitual and preferred register.

Sensitive and effective professional services need not necessarily reject intimate register. Some clients will speak and relate to a professional as a child would to a parent for lack of another professional role model. Without unduly restricting the client's autonomy, a skilled lawyer can assume an appropriately intimate communication voice, meaning one that is frank, sensitive, open, supportive, and caring, but firm and clear in guidance and counseling. To do otherwise may in some circumstances be the worst affront a lawyer could give to a client, which would be to reject the only form of communication with which the client may be familiar, and one that assumes the greatest level of trust and respect. Respect and know intimate register.

Casual Register

Casual register approximates intimate register in the simplicity and informality of its words and grammar, and the familiarity of the relationship between speaker and listener. Casual register depends on the speaker and listener's familiarity with one another or their willingness to treat one another as familiar. Yet casual register assumes a greater level of mental and emotional independence between speaker and listener. Casual register assumes equal terms and footing between speaker and listener.

Individuals often use casual register in informal and personal-acquaintance settings and relationships, particularly to establish or reestablish relationship through common knowledge or experience. Examples can include: "I haven't seen you lately—you must be busy!" "Did you see the game last night?" "So what did you think of your trip to the Caribbean?" Like other language registers, individuals of all education levels and socioeconomic classes occasionally employ casual register on different occasions and in different contexts. Also, as in the case of other language registers, culture, age, sex, education, socioeconomic status, and other factors can influence whether an individual will use casual register. An individual may use casual register in some settings but not others, while other individuals will use casual register in all settings or no settings.

Clients may use casual register in professional settings, particularly at the outset and conclusion of consultations. Professional norms may in some settings call for casual conversation at those or other moments. Other clients may use casual register throughout a consultation or not at all during a consultation. Consider an example.

"Hey, man," the client greeted the lawyer without sitting down in the cubicle provided for them, "I just have a quick question. That alright?"

With an easy, one-shouldered shrug and a light flip of the hand, the lawyer answered, "Sure, what's up?" at the same time making sure to push aside the client intake form and look unoccupied, to acknowledge the casual form and nature of the client's request.

The lawyer intended these actions as signals that the client was free to proceed as casually as the client wished. The lawyer had seen a hundred other clients start with the same offhand "quick question." The client's offhand manner may just have been the client's parry for not yet trusting the lawyer, not knowing a more formal language, or fearing to take his own problem too seriously. The lawyer knew that the problem would probably be as serious as other problems and require just as lengthy of a consultation. Nonetheless, the client clearly needed or preferred to keep things simple and light, perhaps to diminish the ·authoritative in a world where authority may not have treated the client so well.

As the above vignette suggests, a careless lawyer can easily misunderstand a client's use of casual register by misreading the client's deep concern with a serious problem. Do not mistake casual register for casual concern. Using casual register can have different meanings in different situations for different clients. Lawyers should be sensitive to the client and circumstance. For example, a lawyer's use of casual register can be an invitation to the client to trust the lawyer. On the other hand, a lawyer's use of casual register can be a sign to the client (intended or not) of carelessness or lack of respect. A client may studiously and appropriately avoid responding to the lawyer's use of casual register until the client sees other reasons to trust the lawyer.

Similarly, a client's use of casual register may indicate a desire to trust the lawyer. On the other hand, a client's use of casual register may mean (and here the professional must be especially attentive) that the client has limited familiarity with other language registers. When a client uses a casual language register, the lawyer should be especially careful not to employ consultative, formal, or frozen registers without ensuring that the client understands and appreciates their use. Likewise, when the client employs consultative, formal, or frozen language registers, the lawyer should hesitate to use casual register unless the client clearly indicates a willingness to share that register. The point is generally to *match the client's register*. Clients use different registers subconsciously, but registers remain important to the client in the way that they perceive the lawyer's response.

"Chances are, if your organization sends an employee into another country to work, you spend considerable time preparing him to operate in the new culture. But what about employees who have frequent international cross-cultural contact without ever leaving the United States? Too often, training and education for this group is overlooked.

"'Educating your local employees about communicating across cultures is even more relevant today than in the past when it was just about interacting with colleagues on assignment from another country. In today's world, many teams are multinational and use technology to communicate and collaborate as if they were sitting next door to each other,' says C. David Gammel, a Maryland-based business consultant and former founding director of the Center for International Assignment Management, a division of the Employee Relocation Council.

"A report by Robert E. Lewis, Ph.D., for Personnel Decisions International (PDI), a global talent management firm, bears this out.

"'Global work used to occur when managers and executives crossed borders. Now, a finance manager in the Midwest plains of the U.S. can communicate with a vendor in Asia and a customer in Europe without leaving his/her hometown. In a world where software development projects are worked on 24 hours a day as they are shipped from Palo Alto to Bangalore to Dublin the need for workers who can speak in global terms, and managers who can manage in global terms, is profound,' Robert E. Lewis, Ph.D., author of the report, writes.

"Unfortunately, Lewis says, too few employers are preparing employees for the new reality. 'We expect managers and executives to oversee global project teams, call centers, and production via videoconferences and emails with nearly no preparation.'" Maureen Minehan, *Cross-Cultural Training: Not Just for Expatriates Anymore*, 17/1 INT. HUM. RTS. J. Art. 8 (Winter 2008).

Consultative Register

Consultative register draws on the speaker's and listener's knowledge, skills, experience, and other performance-based qualifications. Consultative register should make you think of professional consultations, tending to have a point or purpose associated with the professional's expertise and the client's need for it. Consultative register communicates practical information in a purposeful, pragmatic, means-leading-to-ends mode. Examples of consultative register can include: "Here's what will happen if you make that choice." "Just tell me what you think so that I can decide." "I will help you only if you are willing to listen and accept my advice." "There is nothing else I can offer you."

As in the case of other registers, individuals of all socioeconomic classes may use consultative register in certain settings and at certain times, even though some listeners tend to associate consultative register with middle- to upper-middle socioeconomic (education and income) classes than either lower socioeconomic class or upper socioeconomic class. Speakers use consultative register most often in transactional settings involving bargained exchanges of goods and services rather than in communications based on relationship.

Individuals may also use consultative register in families or in certain relationships within families, although consultative register is likely not the dominant register in casual or intimate settings. Consultative register used between or among certain family members may indicate the dominance of exchange, expertise, or performance over relationship. Individuals may also use consultative register among friends in social or recreational settings, especially if the individuals use consultative register in their field or profession. Listen carefully to lawyers or accountants on the golf course. They may sound more like lawyers or accountants golfing than golfers who happen to be lawyers or accountants. The lawyers may bargain their way around the course under negotiated rules, while the accountants may make more of the scorekeeping, both acting through consultative registers employed commonly in their professions.

Lawyers are quite familiar with consultative register. Indeed, they may be so familiar with consultative register that they fail to recognize that their use of it distinct from other registers. Consultative register is so closely linked to the analytical thinking and skills that lawyers employ that lawyers who use only consultative register in professional settings may not recognize its strengths and weaknesses, and the value of other registers. Consultative register gets to the point or bottom line, which can be its advantage. Yet consultative register can overlook the professional relationship itself, which in some settings may carry more value to the participants than the particular bargained-for exchange. Put simply, for some clients at some times, it means more to have a lawyer than to have the lawyer's advice. Relationship can mean more than exchange.

Be ready to hear yourself using consultative register and to adjust and adapt to other registers, especially when the client seems not to be engaged in and receiving your advice. Recognize that while consultative register can be most effective in identifying objectives and means to obtain them (that kind of instrumental thinking that lawyers learn to practice), it can also be confusing, distracting, cold, and even insensitive to clients who habitually or out of choice employ other registers. Consultative register, when poorly or inappropriately employed, can remove emotion from the voice and compassion from the demeanor of the speaker, strip the listener of dignity, and rob the professional relationship of trust and mutual concern.

An effective lawyer may deliberately choose to use frozen, formal, casual, or intimate registers when the client seems overly focused on means and ends. Clients can benefit from the change in perspective that comes with a change away from consultative register. Consider using casual, formal, or frozen register when a client seems more fixed on exchange than seems prudent and helpful under the circumstances. Clients can benefit from the enrichment that can come from the slight change in perspective accompanying a change in register. The lawyer who can gently, through the use of alternate language registers, help the client gain a fresh perspective on the client's situation may accomplish more by doing so—grant the client greater autonomy and strength—than by keeping the professional relationship purely consultative. To the imaginative intercultural lawyer, the possibilities to embrace and enrich the client's communicative world are endless.

Formal Register

Formal register recognizes roles, achievements, status, education, origins, certifications, and positions. Formal register may make use of titles and honorifics. Formal register depends on the publicly recognized relationship of the speaker and listener, and persons about whom they communicate. A client's use of formal register indicates that the client considers significant the relative status and roles of lawyer and client, not necessarily that the lawyer has a superior status and role but that roles and status are significant to the client who may have status and role that bear on the professional matter.

Examples of formal register may include: "Yes, sir." "Doctor Johnson—may I call you that? Your law degree is a doctorate." "I earned my master's degree from Southern. Where did you go?" "That's an interesting last name. Where is your family from?" "I was a Phi Delta Alpha. You?" "Have you made partner yet?" Consider the following example.

The sprite, older client wore brilliant clothing and a wide-brimmed hat. She set the small bags of food that she had just earned helping out at the soup kitchen on the little round table separating her from the lawyer. Although practically destitute, with bare subsistence means, she extended her hand to the lawyer palm down as a society lady might. The client then gave the lawyer her name insisting that the lawyer get the spelling of her last name—a famous last name that she said the lawyer must have recognized—just right.

The client then spoke briefly of her ancestors and father, while inquiring respectfully of the lawyer's own birthplace and ancestry. Only then, after having satisfied something within her by these formalities (probably including the trust she now had for the lawyer who had welcomed and returned the formalities), did the client gradually share the difficulty that had caused her to seek the legal consultation.

Do not underestimate the value of formal register to lawyer and client. The use of formal register tends to grant honor, invoke authority, and establish relationships through membership and role. Its use by a client may indicate a special willingness to recognize and accept social distinctions as lending stability to relationships. Effective lawyers recognize the value of formal register. A client giving honor to the lawyer or another person through the use of formal language is not an empty act, although the tendency of overly analytical lawyers may be to treat it as such. Formal register is a sign of respect. It can also be a sign that the client wants the lawyer to respect the client in return. If the client insists on calling the lawyer "Mr." or "Ms.," then the client may expect you to address the client alike.

Formal register is also a clue to the way in which a client may prefer to structure relationships with the lawyer and others. The lawyer who can respond to the client in kind may find a basis for trust that the lawyer who is unwilling to use formal register would miss. Lawyers have several ways in which to establish trust, and using an appropriately formal language register is one of them. Formal register may even be a clue to how the client perceives the underlying legal issue, which may have arisen out of a disruption in roles and status. Clients using formal register may be more concerned that the legal system restore rights associated with their status or qualifications than achieve for them specific financial or other materials goals.

Frozen Register

Frozen register uses quoted, memorized, rote, scriptural, or other memorialized language that does not change. Use of frozen register is among the clearest possible indications of the client's experience and commitments. Frozen register reveals identity, beliefs, meaning, commitments, and traditions. Use of frozen register does not depend on education or income. Clients of lower education levels, even illiterate clients, may be just as likely or even more likely to use frozen register than clients of higher education levels.

Individuals of all cultures and socioeconomic classes may use frozen register in certain settings and at certain times. The references clients use in frozen register may be diverse, from popular song to movie scripts, literature, or sacred texts. Examples of frozen register may include: "Aren't all men created equal?" (*Gettysburg Address*). "Let the Lord be my shepherd." (*23rd Psalm*). "He was like Little Jack Horner sitting in the corner!" (*Nursery Rhyme*). "My dad is the salt of the earth." (*Sermon on the*

Mount). "I learned not to lean on my own understanding." (*Proverbs 3:5*).

When using frozen register, the client is intentionally or unintentionally giving the lawyer a clue that the lawyer should value highly. Frozen register can constitute a powerful use of cultural metaphor reflecting a depth and continuity of experience that the client wishes to share with the lawyer. The client's specific frozen reference can lead the lawyer to literary, artistic, scriptural, and other mental, emotional, and spiritual connections and resources to use in the consultation. It can also give clues to the lawyer about the company that the client keeps and society that the client values.

Yet frozen register is also one of the first cultural references that overly analytical lawyers too often reject. Lawyers train in the analytical rather than in analogical and metaphorical (even literary) traditions. It takes a wise lawyer with a sensitive professional identity to draw on analogical, metaphorical, literary, and scriptural traditions when a client's frozen register indicates that the client wishes to do so. Clients do not always think in the analytical. They may think more commonly and more productively in the analogical, by relating their situation to real or imagined stories described in song, movie, literature, or scripture. Those connections can be powerful sources of guidance for clients. Clients can sensibly make meaning of their own lives as stories. Through frozen register, they may be connecting their lives to larger stories of communities, nations, or peoples.

Lawyers need not reject those connections. Client autonomy and respect may require that the lawyer recognize those connections as acceptable bases on which clients will evaluate legal services and options. The lawyer who ignores a reference that a client makes using frozen register may be insulting the client. At the least, clients will notice when lawyers miss their frozen references. Some clients will judge such lawyers to be insensitive, uninformed, or not as wise in the ways of the world as they had hoped. What good is a lawyer who does not know a people's most common references, those that they share in conversation? Be especially sensitive to any use of frozen

110

register. Be ready to acknowledge and embrace its use as a critical reference and resource possessed by your client.

> "Many writers advocate more of a global if not a cosmic consciousness, and we can learn what this is from non-Western systems of thought. Historically, however, we have labeled cultures as retrograde for having a larger cosmology embedded in mythic structures" and in doing so have "established western scientific thinking as superior to the thinking of other existing cultures. [] So-called Western knowledge is a relatively recent phenomenon, first spread through colonization and then through globalization. Anchored in classical Greek thought, the dominance of Western knowledge has resulted in nonattention to, if not outright dismissal of, other systems, cosmologies, and understandings about learning and knowing. Only recently have we witnessed a growing interest in learning as an embodied, spiritual, or narrative phenomenon [], or as something structured by a wholly different worldview. []" Sharan B. Merriam & Young Sek Kim, *Non-Western Perspectives on Learning and Knowing*, in SHARAN B. MERRIAM & ANDRE P. GRACE, CONTEMPORARY ISSUES IN ADULT EDUCATION 378, 379 (John Wiley & Sons, Inc. 2011) (citations omitted).

Matching Register

The above discussion suggests the general value of matching the client's register. When a client speaks in a certain register, it is generally appropriate for the lawyer to reply in the same register. When a lawyer uses the same register in reply, the lawyer exhibits a level of understanding and appreciation for the client including the client's emotional state. The lawyer also shows willingness to adopt the client's relationship preference, from informal to formal. Using a badly mismatched register more than one register away from the client's register can adversely affect the professional relationship. The closer the register, the more likely the client will appreciate the communication.

Approximating but not perfectly matching the client's register may be appropriate. A client may accept that the lawyer responds in casual register to the client's intimate register, or consultative register to the client's casual register. On the other hand, when a lawyer uses a different register, even a register within one degree of separation of the register that the client uses, the client may be somewhat put off or confused. A lawyer's consultative register does not acknowledge the honor a client accords a lawyer by using formal register. A lawyer's casual register may not recognize the seriousness of the client's matter that the client expresses in consultative register or the business basis for the client's use of consultative register.

When a lawyer uses a register two or more degrees of separation from the register the client uses, then the client may readily take offense. The lawyer who does so has clearly rejected the client's communication style and relationship preference. The lawyer who responds in formal register to the client's casual register may be mindlessly indicating to the client that the lawyer is rejecting the client's offer of professional trust and acquaintance.

For another example, a client who during the course of a consultation employs the frozen register—literally quotes from a known source—might reasonably expect the lawyer to acknowledge the known source. In that instance, the lawyer's communication that would most build the client's trust would be for the lawyer to complete or continue the quotation, to acknowledge its source, or if unknown, to inquire of the client in humble appreciation for the client's understanding and resource. Clients, even those who appear to have little education, may have substantial reservoirs of formal material on which to draw. For a lawyer not to acknowledge the client's use of that material is for the lawyer to overlook or reject the client's resource. Clients may use frozen register as a test of the lawyer's willingness to listen to them with care and to adjust the representation to account for the client's commitments and resources. A lawyer who fails or refuses may in the client's view be displaying insensitivity or bias.

To illustrate again, a client who employs an intimate register in the manner of a child speaking to a parent would reasonably expect the lawyer to speak in a similarly intimate register—not as a child, and not (strictly speaking) in the role of a parent, but in the voice or register that a parent would use, which would tend to be simple, direct, familiar, and with beneficent and reassuring authority.

Recognize also that communication registers may change during the course of the client consultation. A client who begins in intimate register by sharing an emotional injury may be testing the lawyer's trust but may quickly move to a casual or consultative register once the client resolves the trust issue. The lawyer who responds to the intimate disclosure of an emotional injury using consultative voice may from the client's view be displaying an emotional insensitivity, a bias against the client's class, or an indication that the lawyer is less than concerned with and appreciative of the client's grievance. The safest action is to match your register to the client's register, using the same register initially and moving to the nearest register only to advance and improve the consultation. You may change registers gradually, but watch for the client's lead, and do not change registers when the client does not appear prepared to do so. Doing so may lead to confusion, loss of trust, and your inability to serve the client.

Reflections

Consider the following exercises in language registers. Record your answers in your journal, and discuss them with another to broaden your views:

1. Identify the register of each of the following client statements in each given circumstance (hint: they follow the order used above from least formal to most formal):

 a. crying, "You don't like me anymore, do you?"

 b. greeting, "Hey, what've you been up to lately?"

 c. concluding, "So, there's my problem. What can you do?"

 d. introducing, "You're a Notre Dame grad, aren't you?"

 e. summarizing, "Heap coals on his head, huh?!"

2. Think of times when you might use each register, intimate, casual, consultative, formal, or frozen, in a typical day in a social setting outside of your professional activities. Rehearse something in each register (intimate, casual, consultative, formal,

and frozen) that you might say in a specific social setting outside of your professional activities.

3. Which was the most common language register used in your family of origin? Which is the most common language register used in your current family? Why do registers differ from family to family?

4. Do the registers that you use within your family differ from family member to family member? If so, then why? What do those differences reveal about the relationships? Can you recall an example of someone's misuse of register negatively affecting personal communication and relationship?

5. What is the language register that you first typically use in a professional setting? Do you change registers from lawyer to lawyer or from lawyer to staff member? Do you use the same register with other lawyers as you do with clients? How do your registers change from professional setting to professional setting?

6. Can you think of an emotionally distraught client who was using intimate register? Do you recall how you responded? Did you use intimate register as a parent might to a child? How did the client respond to your register? Do you feel that intimate register can be appropriate in certain client interactions? Where might it be inappropriate?

7. Do you have clients who commonly use casual register with you? How is your professional relationship with those clients different from clients with whom you do not use casual register? Can you recall an instance when your use of casual register seemed inappropriate in retrospect? In what professional settings would you most avoid using casual register? How might a brief use of casual register be appropriate even in those settings?

8. Do you have a client who uses formal register more frequently than other clients? Can you think of a client with whom you could use formal register to strengthen the relationship? What formal statuses (degrees, licensures, etc.), associations (school, military service, etc.), or roles (parent,

guardian, volunteer, etc.) might you invoke with clients to encourage them with your recognition? How would you most appropriately respond to a client who recognized your status, association, or role, intending to honor you?

9. Can you think of a client who has used frozen register with you? What was the formal reference? How much or little of the reference did you know? How did you respond to the client? What alternative response might have most strengthened the relationship with the client? Why did the client use the reference? What meaning did the reference convey? What did the reference tell you about the client? How might you have used that knowledge in representing the client?

10. Rehearse something that you might say to a client in each register (intimate, casual, consultative, formal, and frozen) in a specific imagined professional setting. Do you see how matching the client's register can be important? Can you see how moving your register one register above or below the client's register could improve or advance the professional consultation?

11. Rehearse something that you would definitely *not* say to a client in each register (intimate, casual, consultative, formal, and frozen) in a specific imagined professional setting. Do you see how mismatching the client's register by two or more registers could harm the client relationship? Can you recall an example of someone's misuse of register negatively affecting professional communication and relationship?

12. Might there nonetheless be instances when you would deliberately and appropriately mismatch the client's register by two or more registers? Can you think of an example when you might want to deliberately mismatch the client's register by two or more registers, to achieve an important professional objective?

Chapter 8

Cognitive

"Write down what he says!"

Thinking Differently

The lawyer stood to greet the client warmly, offering a firm hand, while also acknowledging the counselor who came in with the client. The client shook the lawyer's hand and sat down across from the lawyer at the desk. The client's counselor sat next to the client.

The lawyer and client could hardly have been more different. The lawyer had education, while the client had none. The lawyer had good health, while the client was physically gaunt and broken down, in substance-abuse treatment. The lawyer had good finances, housing, and transportation, while the client was bankrupt, homeless, and restricted to the residential program. The lawyer and client were of different ethnicities, ages, experiences, hopes, and ambitions.

Yet lawyer and client swiftly found an odd bond in the most unlikely of places. As lawyer and client sat down together, the counselor barked impatient orders at the client, "Get out your papers! C'mon, where's your pen? Did you forget it again?" The lawyer and client looked at one another, smiling at the counselor's impatience. The lawyer silently slid his pen across the desk to the client, who smiled and nodded a silent thank you.

The counselor's impatience had already united lawyer and client. They spent the next half hour discussing the series of legal problems that had either dogged the client into substance-abuse treatment or attached like barnacles to him once there. The problems included the usual litany: criminal charges, conviction, probation, and probation violation; mammoth and increasing child-support arrearages; court judgments from credit-card and other debt; suspended driver's license under heavy unpaid fines; and more of the like.

The counselor continued to harangue the client to write down everything that the lawyer said. The client made no such effort, and the lawyer did not want or expect it. The lawyer instead continued to silently evaluate how much and how little the client understood of the lawyer's counsel, and what achievable action the lawyer could identify for the client.

Soon enough, the lawyer had discerned the client's narrow but reasonable path forward. The lawyer drew a second pen from inside his suit coat and started to print large, clear letters on the lined pad before him. The lawyer wrote just three steps, each a declarative one-liner, each with a large number 1, 2, or 3 in front of it. The lawyer then turned the pad respectfully toward the client for the client to attempt to read, while the lawyer read aloud and upside down each step in turn, knowing that the illiterate client was listening and memorizing rather than reading with him. They smiled at one another, both satisfied that they had a plan, and both knowing that the lawyer had simultaneously addressed and silenced the counselor's nagging.

"Now, when you get to three, you come back and tell me how it went, right?" the lawyer ended. The client smiled again, nodded, and extended a warm hand. The counselor barked one last impatient order at the client not to leave behind the lawyer's instructions, which the client was already picking up from the desk and folding into a little square to stuff in his shirt pocket.

Thinking About Thinking

Lawyers have distinct cognitive practices. We are both marvelous at and notorious for discerning goals, setting interim objectives, developing plans, implementing those plans, assessing progress, and adjusting objectives and plans accordingly. Legal education and law practice make these steps just outlined second nature for practicing lawyers. We do it in our sleep, so consistently that we sometimes have to check ourselves after we leave the office and enter the home or engage in other family and social relationships. These cognitive practices are so much of a lawyer's professional identity and so dominant that lawyers sometimes fail to appreciate that clients may not be thinking like them. When clients do not think like lawyers, lawyers may blame them, as the counselor did in the above illustration.

Yet a client's thinking differently may not be due to lack of skill, education, or experience. A client's thinking in other than the lawyer's typical goal-setting, planning, and assessment fashion may instead be due to the client's mental distress, impaired emotions, or the non-professional culture in which the client operates. Clients of diverse educational, socioeconomic, and cultural backgrounds may have different cognitive practices and habits than those that you typically employ or that you recognize in others. Particularly when clients communicate in one of the non-consultative language registers described in the prior chapter, and when they hesitate to articulate clear goals or the willingness to pursue objectives through achievable plans, they may be giving clues to their mental and emotional state, and preferred or presently capable cognitive practices.

For example, a person living in a stable environment, in which specific actions consistently produce specific results, will often think and behave more deliberately than a person living in social chaos where actions do not produce predictable results. Cognition adapts, when cause and effect are inconsistent or unclear. Even when environments are alike, individuals may develop distinctly different ways of thinking about events based on distinctly different social orders or belief systems. For example, the culture in which lawyers operate tends to be as highly individualistic as any culture could be. Clients may instead not be accustomed to think of individual interests and may instead think in broader terms of family and community interests.

Lawyers should be sensitive to alternative cognitive practices, or they may fail to understand, serve, and support diverse clients. Be especially aware that clients employing intimate and casual register in their communications may benefit more by their relationship with you than by the service you hope and expect to give them. Your performance-based, cognitive skills can be helpful to them. Some clients will not possess those planning skills that seem so basic to you. You may be able to help those clients most by making explicit the cognitive steps and skills that they must exercise if they are to benefit from your service.

Yet those performance-based skills are not the only and sometimes not even the most-beneficial services you can give to some clients. Relationship—the trust that develops and respect that lawyer and client exchange in professional consultation—may be more important and more valuable in some instances than the legal counsel and transactional service.

A Cognitive Framework

The prior chapter offered a language-register framework to improve communication skills to serve diverse clients. This chapter offers a second heuristic, this one to help a lawyer develop, improve, and modify cognitive skills when serving diverse clients. The cognitive framework offered here is the one already introduced immediately above. It should be familiar to any lawyer. Lawyers think by (1) discerning goals, (2) setting interim objectives, (3) developing plans to achieve those objectives, (4) implementing those plans, and (5) assessing progress to adjust objectives and plans accordingly until the client reaches or is unable to reach the goal.

The challenge when serving diverse clients is to be more aware of how to articulate the above cognitive framework to a client not familiar with it and then also how to modify it to support diverse clients. Like the consultative language register with which lawyers communicate, a lawyer's standard goal-setting cognitive framework is so powerful that it can inhibit the professional relationship with a diverse client. As you consider the following five cognitive skills, consider also watching for, valuing, supporting, and adapting to clients' different ways of thinking about their legal issues.

"Despite the profession's reluctance to mandate that lawyers bring non-doctrinal issues to the table when giving advice, it seems unlikely that a lawyer fulfills her duty to provide a client with adequately informed assessments of the strengths and weaknesses of alternatives, and to provide reasoned opinions about the relative propriety of various options if she has not factored both legal rules and relevant contextual considerations into her deliberative calculus. Given the prevalence of influences other than rights, powers, and obligations derived from formal legal rules, the notion that lawyer's judgment can be either truly "independent" or "professional" without reference to the potential impact of social, cultural, and structural factors operating within the situation appears untenable." Footnotes omitted. Angela O. Burton, Cultivating Ethical, Socially Responsible Lawyer Judgment: Introducing the Multiple Lawyering Intelligences Paradigm into the Clinical Setting, 11 Clinical L. Rev. 15, 17 (2004).

Discerning Goals

Lawyers see client consultations as having defined point or purpose. Lawyers tend to be ends-oriented achievers and bottom-liners. They may thus assume that clients know what they want if not how to get it. Lawyers tend to think instrumentally, that consultations are means to ends. They may expect clients to do likewise. In the ordinary consultation, a lawyer may reasonably assume that the client knows why the client is seeing the lawyer. Lawyers are quite familiar with helping clients evaluate lawful goals. Clients often come to lawyers with clear goals such as to form a business, obtain a divorce or bankruptcy, prepare an estate plan, obtain an insurance benefit, collect on an overdue account, or defend a lawsuit.

On the other hand, some clients will not have the practice of determining (even implicitly) their goals for consultation with a lawyer. This apparent shortcoming may especially be true for clients who speak primarily or solely in intimate or casual register. Because they are not using consultative register, they are not thinking in consultative (transaction, purpose-based) terms.

Do not assume that clients who fail to articulate clear goals for the consultation are incapable, irresponsible, or lacking in ambition. Sound reasons may explain why a client would not articulate goals. Articulating goals may simply not be common in the client's culture. Openly sharing a strongly held goal may be unwise in the client's community because of the probability that others would discourage the client's pursuit of the goal or even directly oppose and undermine the client's achievement of the goal. Individual goals may imply disrespect of community interests. Individuals may also so seldom obtain goals that announcing them may be unfamiliar or self-defeating.

In cross-cultural consultations, clients may also be waiting to develop trust or rapport with the lawyer before sharing a goal that may be highly personal, private, or revealing. The client's culture may also not distinguish legal matters from medical, financial, social, occupational, and other matters. The cross-culturally effective lawyer should give explicit attention to determining the client's goals. That attention may require explaining to the client that the lawyer will hold the client's matter in strict confidence. It may include helping the client sort law-related goals from health, social, financial, political, and other goals. Consider an example.

By ghastly effect of the substances he was abusing, the homeless young client shivered in the sweltering heat of the soup kitchen's day room as he talked to the lawyer in private consultation. The client's speech was a series of vague grievances, some expressed with greater vehemence than others, as his eyes crossed and wandered under his drugged condition. Yet he was unwilling to allow the lawyer to interrupt to guide him until he had ended his story of property theft, fights, and sleeping at the homes of acquaintances and in cars and under freeway bridges. Finally, the client paused, leaning heavily and unsteadily forward on the little table between them to stare disconcertingly in the lawyer's eyes for answers to questions that the client had not asked in his rambling litany.

The lawyer began gently and with concern, "I can see it's been really hard for you. How do you think I can help?"

The young client, surprised at the lawyer's brevity if not also at the lawyer's kindness and concern, shot back, "How should I know? You're the lawyer."

The lawyer, with growing confidence at how the consultation would proceed, tried again, saying gently, "It seems to me that you are most concerned right now about getting your things out of your ex-friend's residence. Is that right?"

The young client brightened at the thought before responding, at first hesitantly, "Yeah. Yeah. That would really be nice, man."

The lawyer and client spent the next several minutes discussing the practical and legal steps to recover the client's personal property. The lawyer wrote some notes out for the young client, handing him a brochure of legal resources as he left. The lawyer would see the young client several more times over the next couple of years, with the client looking better at times, not much worse at others. The client seemed to recognize in these subsequent consultations not only that the lawyer could actually help with some things but that the client should be thoughtful about what were those goals and objectives. Maybe life could even get better.

An effective lawyer must ensure that the lawyer does not assume or impose goals for the consultation that the client does not have. Lawyers, like other professionals, can readily get in the habit of providing commoditized services, whether those services are divorces, wills, or bankruptcies (to give three examples). Lawyers in the practice of providing commoditized services must be especially careful about imposing objectives on clients while ignoring other client objectives that do not fall within the lawyer's commoditized services. Lawyers can have a wider range of skills than they ordinarily realize. Clients can have a wider range of goals than lawyers realize.

Cross-cultural consultations especially can lack important goal-setting context for both lawyer and client. Culture creates a set of expectations. A lawyer operating within one culture may mistakenly assume that a cross-cultural client shares the same expectations and thus the same goal or objective. The lawyer must ensure that the lawyer explores explicitly with cross-cultural clients just what the clients hope to accomplish through the consultation, without the lawyer assuming context that the clients do not share because of the difference in cultures.

Explore goals patiently. Use questions like "How can I help you?" and "What would you like to see happen?" Above all, listen to the client with care, watching for confusion or hesitation. Avoid demanding that clients articulate goals if they seem unable. Do not assume that your transactional consultation is the only service you have for the client. Avoid statements like, "Well, if you don't know what you want, then I can't help you." Support those clients with alternative formulations like, "I appreciate the trust you've shown in sharing your matter with me. Can you tell me more about why you chose to see me?" Not every consultation will have a clear goal. More than one consultation may be necessary to develop trust and establish context that will soon make it clear how you can help. And then again, sometimes the benefits of consultation are not service-oriented and instrumental. Sometimes, just having a lawyer—someone whom the powerless may admire and respect—listen to the client is sufficient service.

Setting Objectives

Clients achieve large goals by accomplishing smaller interim objectives. Lawyers are good at discerning the objectives that will lead to attaining larger goals. Lawyers know how to break larger goals down into interim steps that will lead a client toward achieving the goals. Lawyers are skilled at listing objectives in the order that will accomplish the larger goal.

Lawyers are also skilled at prioritizing objectives. They discern what tasks a client must accomplish first in order to be able to accomplish some other task later. Lawyers easily develop timelines for the ordered tasks, discerning how long each task or series of tasks will require, determining whether the lawyer can accomplish the goal within the client's required time. By contrast, even if clients can discern that they need to accomplish certain subsidiary tasks, they may still not be practiced at putting them in the necessary order and recognizing which tasks they must accomplish first. Even modest litigation matters like obtaining a name change or expunging a conviction can require many discrete steps taken in specific order.

A lawyer's objective-setting skills are tools and artifacts of the highly independent and instrumental professional culture in which lawyers operate. Not every culture conceives of the individual as so independent or the individual's actions as so driven toward ends. Other cultures, whether national or local, social or professional, may place community above individual and relationship above ends. Clients operating within those alternative cultures may be unaccustomed to discerning objectives. Education, habit, environment, or culture may have prevented or discouraged clients from discerning interim objectives. Clients may have lacked sufficient independence within their community or family, or under their various legal, financial, educational, social, and cultural constraints, to articulate and pursue objectives. Consider the following example.

The lawyer had for several years provided pro bono service to three relatively impoverished communities. Many of the clients whom he served were mentally or physically disabled, without job skills or education, elderly, and on public assistance. They had few or none of the usual means by which individuals accomplish legal and administrative tasks—few or no telephones, computers, email accounts, and vehicles. They had little or no skill using administrative resources. As a consequence, the lawyer did nearly all of the clients' planning and much implementing of the plans. He brought much of the pro bono work back to his office for legal assistants to accomplish through telephone calls, correspondence, faxes, and emails that other clients would on their own have been able to accomplish. The clients seemed relatively helpless, both in planning and executing, which was part of why the lawyer served and enjoyed the service.

Later, the lawyer came to serve a homeless population. He expected to find a similar sort of helplessness but instead found the opposite. The homeless clients often needed little more than some rudimentary information about the law and legal resources, things like how and where to file a small claim and obtain a fee waiver. The lawyer often found the homeless clients to be highly skilled at setting, ordering, and prioritizing objectives. The lawyer guessed that to survive in their environment, the homeless clients had to be skilled at determining what steps to take to accomplish survival goals. The lawyer soon learned to bring a different set of expectations and resources to the consultations with the homeless clients, creating and acquiring note cards, brochures, and other handouts through which the clients could facilitate their own matters.

"Micro-messages are small, 'sometimes unspoken, and often unconscious messages that are constantly sent and received that can have a powerful impact on our interactions with others.'

"Micro-affirmations 'convey inclusion, respect, trust, and genuine willingness to see others succeed.' They may lead to a more productive and efficient work environment where all members feel valued and enjoy work.

"Micro-inequities are the ways in which individuals are either singled out, overlooked, ignored, or otherwise discounted based on an unchangeable characteristic such as race or gender. A micro-inequity usually takes the form in slight difference of language, gesture, treatment, or even tone of voice. They are often subconsciously given but can have a huge impact on a work environment or social structure." American Bar Association, *Building Community Trust: Improving Cross-cultural Communication in the Criminal Justice System* 27 (June 2010) (footnotes omitted), *quoting* LAUREN N. NILE, DEVELOPING DIVERSITY TRAINING FOR THE WORKPLACE: A GUIDE FOR TRAINERS 3-48 (NMCI Pubs. 9th ed. 2008).

Planning to Achieve Objectives

Within their usual consultations, lawyers develop and rely on a set of practices as to the division of labor among lawyer, client, and others, to achieve client objectives. In certain practices and practice areas, like complex civil litigation in a large firm, the lawyers do everything, with the client assuming a passive role. The lawyers have the skill, while the clients have the means to pay the lawyers to exercise it. The clients expect the lawyers to exercise the skill without substantial contribution from the client. In other practices and practice areas, like consumer bankruptcy in a small firm, lawyers and clients divide responsibilities. The lawyers have the skill, but the clients may have the information to organize, or they may lack the resources to pay the lawyers to do everything for them. Lawyer and client develop and communicate expectations as to who will do which tasks.

Culture can also influence expectations as to who will do what to accomplish objectives. Clients may be unfamiliar with professional norms regarding division of labor. They may not understand that they may be able to choose certain tasks to perform or that the lawyer expects them to perform those tasks. They may be unaccustomed to exercising initiative in complex matters. They may also have learned not to exercise that initiative because of lack of success in the past at legal and administrative matters. Do not assume that clients who fail to show planning initiative are lazy or do not care about their matters. They may believe that they lack the skill when instead they possess it. They may believe that they ought to defer to the lawyer as an expert, when instead the lawyer may determine that the client has the skill and should exercise it. Consider the following example.

Although he had his intake and referral forms at the ready for every client, the lawyer always kept a blank, lined pad on the table between him and the client. The client whom the lawyer was serving clearly understood each task the lawyer was describing regarding paternity and child support. Yet the client's questioning showed the lawyer that as soon as they had discussed the first task and turned to the second, the client had little recollection of or confidence in accomplishing the first.

"Let's write this down," the lawyer offered.

"Yeah," the client answered gratefully, adding after a moment's thought, "My daughter can help me."

The lawyer had learned already that the client had a bright eight-year-old daughter. The client's reference to her daughter suggested to the lawyer that the client may be unable to read or have difficulty reading. So the lawyer printed the instructions in large, clear letters, using words the client's eight-year old child could probably read, with big circled numbers in the right order, 1, 2, 3, and 4.

"You come back and see me if any of this doesn't go right, alright?" the lawyer ended.

Lawyers may appropriately list the steps a client needs to take to obtain an objective. When doing so for a client who is unfamiliar with the practice of planning, lawyers should be literal to ensure that steps are clear, complete, prioritized, and memorialized (usually written down) in a manner on which the client can rely. With clients who appear by their confusion or frustration not to be capable of conceptualizing a plan, lawyers may appropriately name only one (the first) step and request that the client return when that the client completes that step. Lawyers may also encourage clients to seek social support from a friend or family member who is an experienced planner.

Do not misattribute confusion over a plan as carelessness or unwillingness to see a legal problem addressed. Detailed planning may be an unfamiliar and otherwise unnecessary practice for certain clients.

Implementing the Plan

In their usual practice, lawyers may reasonably expect that clients will implement plans that lawyer and client have together developed. Clients more often meet expectations when lawyers and clients share cultural context. Well-laid plans seldom go awry when lawyer and client enjoy trusting relationship, shared language, equivalent resources, and sound communication.

Some clients, particularly in cross-cultural consultation, may not implement plans developed with their lawyer. Particularly in cross-cultural consultations, lawyers should not assume that clients who fail to implement and persevere in plans are lazy or disinterested. Lawyers should also not assume that the consultation has had no value to the client simply because the client chooses not to pursue plans that lawyer and client together developed. Consider an example.

"So how are you today?" the lawyer asked the familiar young client. The client had been seeing the lawyer each week now for several weeks. The lawyer avoided asking about any specific matter because the consultations over the client's many small legal matters had not yet produced any result or action. The client could have resolved several of the client's small legal issues but had not attempted to do so.

The client shrugged, answering, "Still don't have my things back. But that's okay." The client was no longer shivering as he had been when he first met the lawyer. The client also seemed to have gained a few spare pounds on his previously gaunt frame.

"So what are you up to?" the lawyer continued quickly in an indirect vein to encourage the client, without putting the client off for not having any particular reason for the consultation. The lawyer added, "You're looking good."

"I made out an application for a job program," the young man volunteered. The client's statement had nothing to do with any legal matter. The statement seemed to the lawyer like a child exhibiting pride before a parent or what one friend might say to another over some good news.

The lawyer smiled broadly, held up his hand, and slapped the client's hand when offered to him, saying, "That's great. There's something out there for you so long as you go get it." The lawyer and client laughed at the lawyer's statement. The client left a couple of minutes later without having brought up any of the several legal matters that lawyer and client had discussed over the previous several visits.

Clients of other environments and cultures may have a variety of reasons, not immediately apparent to their lawyer, as to why they do not follow what appears to the lawyer to be a reasonable plan. Clients may lack the resources (mental, emotional, financial, transportation, social, etc.) that the plan requires. The lawyer may have misunderstood the client's true goal or objective. As in the case of the young client above, the client may benefit more from having a plan than in implementing it. Plans can provide clients with important mental and emotional resources like hope, ambition, interest, standing, and relationship. The client's lack of initiative may also be that the client correctly recognizes or unwisely fears that the goal the plan will achieve, though laudable, will have undesirable effects that will result in a net loss rather than gain for the client.

Lawyers should not blame clients in these situations. They should not consider the planning a failure or end the professional relationship solely on that basis. Even if there are no real obstacles and the client can readily accomplish the plan that the lawyer has laid out for the client, the fact of the consultation and of the professional relationship may be more important to the client than the accomplishment of the plan the lawyer has helped to articulate.

Assessing Plan Progress

Lawyers must account to clients, firms, courts, opposing counsel, agencies, and others for the value and appropriateness of their actions. You seldom find a lawyer doing the same worthless, frivolous, burdensome, or harassing activity repeatedly. Law, conduct rule, and the economics of law practice all discourage it. As a result, lawyers are usually effective at assessing plan progress and altering plans when necessary to achieve their objective. Day to day, hour by hour, lawyers constantly evaluate whether their actions are producing the results that they expected. Lawyers are experts at assessment. Lawyers constantly change their actions as they see that the results are not what will achieve the objective. Assessment is an innate and extraordinarily valuable skill for lawyers, exercised constantly without explicit thought as to its necessity and value.

By contrast, some clients, and particularly those whom a lawyer serves in cross-cultural interaction, may not have the practice, habit, or skill of assessing plans as they implement them. Clients who are unfamiliar with professional relationships may not clarify, adjust, change, or reverse plans when appropriate. Clients may lack the confidence, understanding, or other cultural context to know when and what they can change in plan implementation. They may persist in an assigned task trusting or assuming that the lawyer expects them to do so. Lawyers should support those clients with that assessment. You may find it necessary in cross-cultural service to anticipate, discuss, and plan for assessment, when in your usual practice you could reasonably assume that the client would not need counsel regarding assessment. Consider an example.

"Good to see you again," the lawyer greeted the client in the office above the soup kitchen, "How's it going?" The client had already unfolded the lawyer's instructions, written about a month earlier, from a wad of personal papers that the client was carrying wrapped in a plastic sack inside a backpack.

"I don't know," the client responded in a resigned and irritable fashion, "Nothing seems to work." The lawyer had encouraged the client to return within a month and so was glad to see that the client had done so. The lawyer had developed a habit of ending every one of these soup-kitchen consultations with an estimate of the time the client's task should take and encouragement for the client to return after that time.

The lawyer and client sat down at the table and began together to review each step in the lawyer's written instructions. When they were done, the lawyer had written some modifying detail on the instructions. The client folded the paper back up along its well-worn creases and put it back in the little plastic sack with all of the other worn and folded papers. The client seemed rejuvenated to tackle the task.

If a client seems unable to follow a plan, then the lawyer should help the client reconsider the steps and instructions. The lawyer should also ensure that the lawyer properly drew and prioritized the plan, and that each step the client had so far taken had achieved the intended interim result. Legal matters can seem simple to a lawyer who has handled them for many years, when instead the steps necessary to address them are numerous, discrete, and complex. For example, to simply instruct a client in a pro se matter to "file a motion" ignores the complexity of drafting, obtaining a hearing date, and filing and serving notice of the motion. Even as simple of an act as serving an opposing pro se party can involve several steps including copying, mailing, completing a certificate of service, and timely filing the certificate.

When a client fails to implement a plan, the lawyer should also ensure that the client has not perceived a defect in the plan or even in the goal or objective. Lawyers can help clients with these assessments and with goal, objective, and plan modifications that will enable and empower the client while preserving client dignity and autonomy.

Clients caught in unsuccessful cross-cultural representations may grow as frustrated as you grow. Do not mistake client frustration over not being able to execute your properly drawn plan as a challenge to your legal skill and knowledge, even when the client attributes frustration to your purported incompetence. Keep matters professional, not personal. Your pride is not important. Instead, help the client assess the plan's progress. Show optimism where optimism is appropriate. Find a new way to express or execute the plan. Develop a different and better plan where your professional judgment indicates that the plan may in fact not succeed because of the client's unwillingness or inability.

Reflections

Consider the following reflections on the above framework for supporting a client's cognitive skills in cross-cultural service. Add these reflections to your journal. Find an acquaintance with whom to discuss these questions, or organize a group discussion, to broaden and enrich your view:

1. Recall an instance when you articulated a goal but, as you worked toward achieving that goal, you realized that you had chosen the wrong goal. What led you to that realization? Did you benefit from anyone's counsel? Did you abandon the goal completely, or did you simply modify the goal into a related goal?

2. Recall an instance when you worked with another person on a joint task for a time before realizing that you and the other person had different goals. How did you discover that your goals differed? What did you do once you made that discovery? Can two or more work together having different goals?

3. Think of a community to which you belong. Then, articulate one major goal that the community has. Then, articulate your primary individual goal in being a member of that community. Does your individual goal detract from or conflict with the community's goal? Can you think of an instance when you withdrew from a group or community because your individual goals differed from the community's goals? Can you think of an instance when you sacrificed an individual goal for the goals or betterment of a community of which you were a member?

4. Recall an instance when a situational constraint prevented you from completing an assigned or expected task, but you were blamed instead for a lack of interest, skill, or motivation. How did you feel about the person who blamed you wrongly? Did it change your relationship with that person? Why did the person attribute you not having completed the task to your fault rather than to the situation?

5. On a scale of 1 to 10 with 10 being the best or highest, rate your capability on each of the following cognitive skills: (a) articulating goals; (b) setting objectives; (c) planning to achieve objectives; (d) implementing plans; and (e) assessing and modifying plans according to progress.

6. Choose a professional acquaintance, personal friend, or family member whom you know well, and rate that person on the same scale of 1 to 10 as to each of the following skills: (a) articulating goals; (b) setting objectives; (c) planning to achieve objectives; (d) implementing plans; and (e) assessing and modifying plans according to progress.

7. Identify a professional acquaintance, personal friend, or family member who you feel is stronger than you at each of the following skills and on whom you would rely for advice or support: (a) articulating goals; (b) setting objectives; (c) planning to achieve objectives; (d) implementing plans; and (e) assessing and modifying plans according to progress.

8. For each of the following skills, identify a professional acquaintance, personal friend, or family member who you feel lacks that skill: (a) articulating goals; (b) setting objectives; (c)

planning to achieve objectives; (d) implementing plans; and (e) assessing and modifying plans according to progress. How might you go about advising that person to support them in using that skill?

9. Think of two questions that you would ask a client to help the client articulate a goal. How would you explain to a client why setting goals for the representation can be helpful? Under what terms would you consult with a client who articulated no specific goal for the consultation? Articulate three benefits that could accrue to a client from consulting with you even if the client had no specific goal for the consultation.

10. Identify five criteria that would help you ensure that you and a client in a cross-cultural consultation have developed an appropriate plan to achieve the client's goal. To help you get started, consider the first criterion to be that you have written down the plan and the last criterion to be that you have prioritized the steps in the plan.

11. Identify four situational or environmental reasons (as opposed to client attributes) why a client might not be implementing a plan. Accept as a first example to help you get started that the client has realized that the client chose the wrong goal.

Chapter 9

Referential

"I am blessed. And you?"

Variation in References

The lawyer met the pro bono client in a cubicle off of the soup kitchen's day room where patrons could get identification, locker, haircut, mail, and shower, and use the washer and dryer. The weary, homeless client responded to the lawyer's "How are you?" greeting with the answer, "I'm blessed. And you?"

The lawyer responded in kind, noticing and appreciating the slight difference, "I'm blessed" rather than "I'm fine," in the client's response. The consultation then ensued over child support that had accumulated while the client was incarcerated for more than a decade.

At the consultation's conclusion, the client rose and extended his hand to the lawyer appreciatively but wearily. As the client turned toward the door to go, the client muttered something that the lawyer barely heard, to the effect of, "Now if I can just make it through the night."

"Tell me," the lawyer rejoined. The client, still pausing at the door but now turned back toward the lawyer, said simply that he was more concerned about the drugs and prostitutes tempting him outside on the streets. The client was not complaining but just making a brief plea without expectation that the lawyer would respond.

Just then, the lawyer remembered how the client had greeted the lawyer. So as the client turned again to leave, the lawyer said simply, "There is no temptation except that which is common to man."

The client stopped, turned back, brightened noticeably, and completed the verse, "And God is faithful; he will not let you be tempted beyond what you can bear. But when you are tempted, he will also provide a way out so that you can stand up under it." The client then explained to the lawyer that he had not thought of the powerful Bible verse since his release from prison 10 weeks earlier. The client now had no doubt that he would make it sober another night—maybe a greater victory for the client and community than anything else the lawyer and client had accomplished that day.

Noticing References

Listen carefully to clients, especially in cross-cultural situations. Watch their actions and expressions with care. You will find that they often deviate in slight ways from what you would expect to observe in other clients. The hints that cross-cultural clients leave for the finely attuned ear and observant eye can suggest important commitments and distinctions. A seemingly offhand reply "I am blessed" may be a quiet declaration of faith. The lawyer who thinks that response weird misses that it may represent a highly developed ethic having potentially important consequences to the consultation.

Cross-cultural clients bring with them different commitments, expectations, and experiences that together can take the shape of a distinct belief system or worldview. Worldviews influence thought and behavior powerfully. A client's worldview may inform the client's beliefs about cosmology (the origin and nature of the universe), epistemology (how we think), ontology (the nature of existence), axiology (how we conceive of relationship), and teleology (what is our purpose). Do not underestimate the significance of worldview and its variety.

Many lawyers share cultural references, belief systems, and worldviews. Legal education offers a relatively uniform professional framework through which lawyers learn to view and interpret events. It must do so to be useful in preparing lawyers for professional practice with one another. The cases and commentary that lawyers share also tend to reflect that distinct professional worldview. Many lawyers also share non-legal sources, particularly news media but also books, art, film, and other cultural resources.

Yet the worldview of lawyers may be distinct from that of clients, particularly in cross-cultural settings. Clients draw perspectives and worldviews from sources outside of legal education and law resources. Clients may also draw perspectives and worldviews from outside of the popular culture with which many lawyers are most familiar. A client's cultural reference points may be so different from that of the law profession that the client may have little or no affinity for the lawyer's worldview.

Clients communicate their reference points, belief systems, and worldviews through both overt and subtle statements and behaviors. Explicit or implicit references can, like the language registers discussed in an above chapter, give clues to those perspectives. Clients communicate with context. You may imagine language to be bereft of reference. Indeed, lawyers tend to communicate in consultation with fewer context statements than do lay persons. Lawyers train to think instrumentally. They pare their language of reference to focus on objectives. In doing so, lawyers subtly assume a professional worldview or perspective. Some clients also communicate with low context. Their words reflect little of their experience, commitment, and culture. They may wholly accept and adopt the professional perspective that the lawyer offers.

Yet other clients, particularly those in cross-cultural settings, communicate with high context, rich with reference. A high-context communicator may mention many things in passing that the typically low-context lawyer may think irrelevant. Cross-cultural consultations naturally tend to generate more client context statements than do consultations where the lawyer and client share the same culture. Cross-cultural clients attempt to communicate to the lawyer their distinct perspective. They may do so only in jest or in an offhand manner so as not to disrupt the consultation or confuse the lawyer. Yet those offhand references may include significant data regarding the client's distinct worldview. To the client, those context statements may not be at all irrelevant and may instead be overt or implicit declarations of commitments. Those references may reflect the client's different manner of conceptualizing the world and identifying its salient features.

> "A woman walks into your office for a divorce consultation. You begin by asking her to describe her family and living situation, income, and marriage. Her story is not unusual....
>
> "You probe further and ask where they got married. She tells you they were married on a reservation in Northern Wisconsin where they lived until early this year. Upon further questioning, the woman explains that she is a member of the Lac Du Flambeau Tribe of Chippewa Indians as are her children, but that her husband is not Native American. She describes herself as a 'traditional Indian' who is very religious and devoted to her cultural heritage, which her husband rejects. She wants custody of her children so that she may raise them to embrace their tribal traditions and knows that her husband will not agree.
>
> "You decide to take the case, but realize there may be Native American cultural issues that will affect its outcome. After some cursory research, you find that not only does jurisdiction come into question, but that Native American cultural traditions may conflict with mainstream 'American' norms built into the family law judicial system. It is your job to educate the judge as to tribal law as it affects jurisdiction and any relevant cultural heritage issues.
>
> "Cases that contain cultural issues, particularly those unfamiliar to mainstream courts, can be challenging for lawyers, judges, and clients. ... To represent your client fully, you must educate yourself, the judge, and your client on issues of law and culture that are germane to the case. In so doing, your role may shift from advocate to educator and back several times during the course of the case.
>
> "Depending on your client's heritage and the circumstances of the case, many tools are available to you in educating the court, such as written memorandum, treatises, and expert witnesses. However, the most important tool in your arsenal is you. Immerse yourself in your client's culture and heritage and any relevant laws. You must make yourself sufficiently knowledgeable on the subject of your client's heritage and the relevant law to present and maintain your client's case." Holly Kuschell Hayworth, *Making the*

Cross-Cultural Case: *Educating the Judge About Race, Religion, and Ethnicity*, 1/4 GP SOLO LAW TRENDS & NEWS (ABA Aug. 2005).

A Worldview Framework

As is true for lawyers discerning differences in client communication and cognition, lawyers also grow more effective in cross-cultural service when they have a framework or heuristic to discern clients' distinct reference systems or viewpoints. A worldview framework can help the lawyer quickly turn rough clues into educated guesses and assembled meanings. Even low-context communicators will give helpful worldview clues, especially if the lawyer has a worldview framework and is willing to inquire of the client with sensitivity. Sometimes, the clue takes just one word, especially if the lawyer has a well-developed worldview framework. Consider an example.

The narrator of the *Planet Earth* television series makes an important cultural reference when she intones in that dry seriousness typical of the secular worldview and television genre that "luck" kept the sun/earth relationship stable over billions of years. A lawyer making a similar comment "weren't you lucky!?" about a certain event related to the client's matter may appear to the client to be foolish, without faith, and insensitive to the client's faith, when the client regards the event as so improbable as to be clearly providential. To some clients, *luck* is a naïvely superstitious attribution that the client and other members of the client's culture and community explicitly reject. Those clients may continue with the representation but do so believing the lawyer to be without faith important to positive outcomes.

A worldview framework can help you be sensitive to the diversity of your clients' reference points, belief systems, and worldviews. Avoid taking the stance that your worldview is necessarily superior to that held by the client. If you do believe your worldview to be superior, then recognize that the client's worldview may nonetheless provide the client with greater resources and inclusion within the client's community. As in the case of communication and cognition, self-knowledge about one's own worldview can be an important step toward cross-cultural competence.

Identify your cultural references, belief system, and worldview from among those discussed below. Then try to appreciate how distinct your worldview may be from the worldview held by some of your cross-cultural clients. Consider as a framework the following several worldviews through which clients may interpret and evaluate events. Find ways to help your clients recognize, preserve, and draw on their cultural references, belief systems, and worldviews. Do not assume that your cross-cultural client shares your worldview or, if not, should adopt yours. Different worldviews have different strengths in different situations. The discussion below is only a start to a rich store of reference.

Therapeutic

Some clients (and lawyers) see the world primarily through a therapeutic model. They speak and act on the basis of their mood or affect, and the strength or absence of their feelings. Their primary concern is with their own psychological or emotional state and with how relationships, circumstances, events, and options *make them feel.* When clients operate from a therapeutic worldview, they first consider how certain relationships, actions, or events make them feel and then shape their behavior accordingly. Statements from therapeutic thinkers include "I feel strongly about this," "They don't care about my feelings," and "I don't like that," as self-justifying rationales for positions, interests, decisions, and actions.

Lawyers who recognize when clients are using sensual and emotional responses consistent with therapeutic thinking to govern their choices and behaviors can adapt advice to take account of the clients' therapeutic reference system. A lawyer might appropriately ask a therapeutic-thinking client, "How would pursuing that legal claim make you feel?" or "Have you thought about how you might feel after you take those actions?" Inquiries focused on the client's feelings can help the client evaluate options and consequences from their therapeutic worldview. By first explicitly considering the client's feelings, a lawyer can also encourage the client to consider other factors that may have more to do with resolving the client's legal problem. The lawyer who ignores feelings and emotions in cross-cultural consultation risks rejection. The lawyer who acknowledges them gains a foothold with the client. Consider an example.

"She had no right to do what she did to me," the client nearly shouted to the lawyer, "We would both feel better if she just left me alone." The client scrunched up her nose and showed her teeth in what seemed to the lawyer to be a caricature of fury. Yet as the client explained the official's actions toward her and her child that had so enraged the client, the lawyer discerned that those actions, apparently so unfamiliar to the client, were instead probably ordinary and likely compelled by official duty.

The lawyer first helped the client regain control over her emotions, which had increased in intensity the more that the client explained her legal situation. The lawyer acknowledged the client's emotional condition, saying, "I can see how angry and frustrated you are. You must feel awful. First tell me how you have managed things feeling like you do, and then we'll talk about what we might do about it to make you feel better."

The client for the first time looked squarely at the lawyer in silence. She continued to squint and blink her eyes rapidly as her rage subsided. Her hands still shook the papers she was holding, and her face was still flush from her elevated heart rate. Yet her rapid-fire accusations against the official had now stopped, even though the lawyer had actually told her to continue to speak about her feelings. The lawyer could see that his first sensitivity had worked. He had recognized the client's therapeutic perspective on her legal matter. Her legal issue had made it difficult for her to function mentally and even physically. The lawyer's verbalizing that recognition to the client had helped the client.

The lawyer adjusted his seat gently and slowly took a deep breath, just loudly and deliberately enough for the client to notice. The client silently mimicked the lawyer's calming actions. Only then did the lawyer break the surprising silence, saying, "You must not want to continue this way." The lawyer then turned again to the client's goal, adding, "What options shall we discuss?"

With each of the actions that the lawyer and client considered, the lawyer was careful to ask the client whether those actions would make the client feel worse or better. Yet with some of the options, the lawyer also asked the probability of a productive result, how her child would feel, how the official might respond, and whether the action would improve the relationship with the official whom the lawyer knew would not be going away.

By acknowledging the client's feelings, a lawyer accepts a client's therapeutic worldview. By exploring other bases for decision-making, the lawyer helps the client address root issues that may be affecting the client's mood and interfering with the client's accomplishment of the client's critical objective to feel better. Feelings are legitimate. They can affect a client's mental, emotional, and physical health, not to mention the client's willingness to listen to the lawyer, and process and benefit from the lawyer's advice.

Yet feelings can also be unpredictable and overly subjective. At their worst, they can rule a person. Uncontrolled feelings can make for unstable relationships and unwise choices. Lawyers should be aware of the benefits and potential detriments of therapeutic thinking. A lawyer in consultation may appropriately offer clients a wider range of bases for making decisions. The legal system is not based entirely or even largely on how clients feel about rights and obligations. Some officials might frankly tell such clients to "get over it." When a lawyer knows the power and limitations of therapeutic thinking, the lawyer can provide a therapeutic-thinking client better service.

Providential

Some clients (and lawyers) see the world as providential in design rather than constructed to be therapeutic. Those clients evaluate events and actions against the world's beneficent design more so than by feelings or similar therapeutic or psychological concepts. When clients operate from a providential reference point, they construct their attitudes and behaviors and relate the attitudes and behaviors of others to beneficent rules and patterns. Providential thinkers tend to see events as unfolding consistent with everyone's welfare including their own to the extent that they act consistent with that providence.

Lawyers are not necessarily by education and training providential thinkers. Clients who share a lawyer's professional culture are also likely not exercising a prominently providential worldview. By contrast, clients in cross-cultural consultation may more commonly be using providential reference systems. The non-lawyer public may hold a significantly higher percentage of individuals of providential faith than does the law profession. Lawyers can recognize providential-thinking clients. Statements from providential thinkers may include, "It was time that happened to him," "I guess I had it coming," and "Isn't that the way the world works?" Lawyers can also help providential-thinking clients draw on their reference system. Providence can be a powerful resource, particularly to cross-cultural clients whose understanding and commitment to a providential faith is deeper than their embrace of a professional's secularism. Consider an example.

"No, I don't think I want to do that," the client kept telling the lawyer. To the lawyer, what the lawyer was proposing had seemed the obvious action. The client was instead having some difficulty or showing some reluctance in expressing why not.

The client just kept saying things like, "I just don't think it is the right time" and "It will all work out." The client was quite satisfied that the lawyer had explained what the client could do as a legal right. Yet soon it became obvious to the lawyer that the client was not going to do what the lawyer reasonably proposed.

Only gradually did the lawyer realize that the client might have had in mind larger concerns. Sometimes, understanding one's legal rights is an important ingredient, even if providential considerations keep one from exercising them. "You know, you have several months before you need to make any decision whether to take legal action," the lawyer concluded.

"Thank you," the client said, "I knew you'd understand. I've been so blessed and know that you will be, too. I may need help later, and I'll let you know." The client rose and offered the lawyer a grateful hand. The lawyer accepted the handshake, for the first time believing that the client may have been making the right choice after all.

Lawyers who recognize when clients are using providential reasoning to govern their choices and behaviors can adapt advice to take account of the clients' reference system. Lawyers and clients should discuss legal rights and actions. Yet a lawyer should not assume that legal action is the client's only appropriate course. A lawyer might appropriately suggest that pursuing a legal claim may be what someone else would do, while asking the client whether the client wants to discuss other options. Generating options that go beyond the instrumental legal course can support a client who perceives the possibility of providential design and beneficence.

Probabilistic

Some clients (and lawyers) see the world primarily as probabilistic. They believe that events happen by chance. When clients operate from a probabilistic standpoint, they consider how statistically likely it will be that certain events occur. They evaluate options and actions based on the probability of predicted results. Like therapeutic and providential worldviews, probabilistic thinking reveals itself in a client's language. Statements from probabilistic thinkers may include "What are the odds of that?" and "It was just my turn—bad luck." The operative question for probabilistic thinkers involves measuring the risk and uncertainty of pursuing various courses of action.

The topic of *luck* is a voodoo variant or distortion of probabilistic thinking. It assumes that supernatural qualities *good luck* and *bad luck* exist and that they influence probabilities. Indeed, to some probabilistic thinkers, the quality can be either positive as in good luck, negative as in bad luck, or fatalistic as in "just my luck." Lawyers may occasionally speak light-heartedly or off-handedly regarding luck. Clients who are probabilistic thinkers may appreciate those comments. Clients who instead hold a providential view and face a serious matter may not appreciate a lawyer's wishes of "good luck" to the same degree as probabilistic-thinking clients.

Probabilistic thinking can be highly valuable to lawyers and clients. Probably (pun intended), we all think to some degree in probabilistic terms. Weighing probabilities of outcomes, whether for example in settlement negotiations, motion hearings, or jury deliberations, helps clients choose between options. Probabilistic thinking though also has its limits. The client who consistently accepts risks will soon realize some of them and eventually realize all of them. A client's probabilistic thinking can undermine others' confidence in the client when some of the risks were inappropriate, no matter how small their chances. Consider an example.

"Really? That's not what I hear," the client responded to the lawyer's caution, "I figured it's only 1 out of 10 that I end up there." The lawyer had been trying to get the client to appreciate the possible outcomes of the upcoming hearing and to consider how to plan for and address them. "Can't you just tell me my chances?" the client asked again.

The lawyer had been reluctant to make predictions because the lawyer was sure that the lawyer had heard only a small part of the relevant facts. "Look," the lawyer finally said with a chuckle, "the best I can do is to tell you that from what I can see, the chances of any one of those three alternatives happening are 50/50."

The client laughed along with the lawyer, appreciating the lawyer's subtle probabilistic humor that three equal alternatives would make for one-out-of-three rather than one-out-of-two odds. "Yeah, right," the client agreed, "and what good are those odds to anyone?"

"Now you've got it," the lawyer encouraged the client, adding, "Let's think about some other options outside of going to hearing." The lawyer and client spent the rest of the consultation developing a settlement proposal that met the client's goals without the uncertain risks of a judge's imposed resolution.

Lawyers who recognize when clients are using probabilistic reasoning to govern their choices and behaviors can adapt advice to take account of the clients' reference system. Lawyers might appropriately suggest, "It seems to me that you have a better than even chance of success" or, "Let's talk about what actions would give you a stronger likelihood of that result." Yet as the above example illustrates, reliable probabilistic thinking depends on reliable information, which clients may not have or be willing to share even with (or especially with) their lawyer. Limiting a consultation to probabilities may also unduly constrain the client's perspective only to options that carry risk, when a lawyer and client may be able to develop risk-free options.

A lawyer may also suggest alternative bases for evaluating client options and actions. A lawyer might in certain cases appropriately rejoin, "You may be right that you have a chance of avoiding responsibility by taking that course, but you might also think about whether the action is in itself right—something that you would want your opposing party to do to you." A life lived purely or primarily by the odds can end up having been a life of greater than necessary uncertainty and hazard, or a life with less meaning and fewer and weaker relationships than the client would have desired if aware of alternative reference systems.

"The social cognition literature on bias warrants detailed exploration. Using a variety of experimental methods, cognitive scientists have exposed a significant divergence between our reports—to others and to ourselves—of our attitudes toward outsiders and the subconscious operations of our minds. Perhaps the best known of these experimental devices is the Implicit Association Test (IAT), which measures implicit attitudes toward or associations with a range of social categories. The IAT, which is available online, and highly worth the time to take, reveals widespread implicit bias against many social groups.... Those findings of implicit or automatic bias often conflict with the self-reported attitudes and beliefs of the test-takers. Indeed, results sometimes reveal implicit bias against groups to which subjects themselves belong." Ascanio Piomelli, *Cross-Cultural Lawyering by the Book: The Latest Clinical Texts and a Sketch of a Future Agenda*, 4 Hastings Race & Poverty L.J. 131, 172 (2006).

Moral

Some clients (and lawyers) see the world from a moral standpoint of right and wrong. They evaluate legal issues and advice on the conviction that they should conduct themselves in a manner fitting to individuals' equal and inherent value. When clients operate from a moral reference point, they consider whether certain actions are right or wrong, meaning whether those actions fit the nature and relationships of the persons those actions will affect.

Lawyers also think morally insofar as law is fundamentally moral. Lawyers may on the other hand accentuate instrumental considerations over moral ones when advising individual clients. The individual-ends-driven nature of much legal service can encourage lawyers to consider individual interests over broader moral concerns. Lawyers may thus often encounter clients whose thinking is more dominantly moral than the lawyer's thinking, especially in cross-cultural consultations with the client unfamiliar with professional culture. Indeed, cross-cultural clients may resist, condemn, and depart from lawyer culture on no point more so than moral considerations.

Lawyers can recognize clients who hold moral worldviews, just as they can recognize clients who are therapeutic, providential, or probabilistic thinkers. Statements from moral thinkers may include "I want to do the right thing," "that is just wrong," "that doesn't look right," and "what's the right thing for this relationship?" A client's effort to discern the duties and expectations for archetypical roles and relationships (father, mother, adult child of an elderly parent, business partner, etc.) may indicate moral thinking.

For clients holding a moral viewpoint, the choice of alternative legal courses of action often depends on identifying the overarching standard or principles dictating right action. Moral clients may resist easy, convenient, or commonly accepted options where those options are inconsistent with principles governing right action. Moral clients may also seek to preserve and promote the virtuous character of the lawyer, client, and individuals with whom the client deals. Consider an example.

"You know, I've been thinking about my mother a lot lately," the client finally admitted to the lawyer after a long consultation that had produced no decision or action. The client added, "I've been wondering what she would have said if she knew what I was going to do."

The client's statement stunned the lawyer. The client was a college-educated former small-business owner. He had recently been released from prison and faced several complex legal and practical challenges. The lawyer, appreciating the client's relative sophistication in legal matters, had been helping the client weigh and predict the chances of succeeding or failing in certain objectives depending on which of several courses the client took, when none of them had looked too promising. The thought had never occurred to the lawyer that the client might just want to do the *right thing*, no matter the probable consequences. The lawyer had not even noticed that the client had mentioned that his mother had died while he was in prison. The lawyer had overlooked an important clue to the client's thinking.

"What would your mother want you to do right now?" the lawyer asked, for the first time recognizing and affirming the client's moral inclination and perspective. As soon as the lawyer asked the question, both the lawyer and client recognized the answer. The client dropped and shook his head, then looked up again at the lawyer with a confident smile. Both lawyer and client knew that the client's course would not be easy. Yet they both also knew that it was the right course for the client.

Lawyers who recognize when clients are using moral reasoning can adapt advice to take account of the clients' reference system. For example, a lawyer might appropriately ask whether the option under consideration is right or wrong. Therapeutic, probabilistic, and instrumental considerations can also hold value to moral-thinking clients. Yet questions of right and wrong can prove powerful bases for addressing actions. By considering the broader fitness of actions to human nature and relations, lawyers and clients can together ground decisions in more stable conceptualizations than individual circumstances often allow. Choosing a series of easy or convenient routes can lead to tougher choices later. Moral actions may prove initially difficult but provide sound and convenient footing later. The lawyer should be prepared to help a client draw on moral considerations, particularly when the client indicates that they embrace moral perspectives and when the client's situation is so complex or seemingly hopeless that morality provides the only sound guide.

"A key strength of objective cultural knowledge is its usefulness in establishing rapport with people from other cultures. Negotiators who learn others' languages can readily demonstrate their interest in others' cultures and begin the rapport-building process directly, without need of interpreters. Likewise, negotiators familiar with their counterparts' legal and political institutions, as well as their history, literature, music, and art, can quickly begin to establish rapport and earn their counterparts' trust. Negotiators who lack objective knowledge of their counterparts' cultures may find it more difficult to build rapport and earn trust.

"Objective cultural knowledge also enhances negotiators' awareness of their counterparts' potential sensitivities. If negotiating with Latin Americans, for example, knowledgeable Texas negotiators may choose to refer to the country in which they live as the 'United States' rather than 'America,' as Latin Americans also consider themselves residents of America. Likewise, knowledgeable Texas negotiators are not surprised when their Latin American counterparts refer to them as 'North Americans' rather than 'Americans,' as Latin Americans believe most people who live in the Western Hemisphere are Americans.

"While objective cultural knowledge is useful, it has limitations. No negotiator can become completely knowledgeable about the objective cultural aspects of every society. In fact, negotiators generally must limit their quest for objective cultural knowledge to the types of people with whom they interact most frequently. In addition, it is possible to acquire in-depth knowledge of certain aspects of objective culture (history, government, geography) without acquiring any effective skills in communicating or negotiating with people from that culture. Knowledge of objective culture, to be effective, must be combined with knowledge of subjective culture." Walter A. Wright, *Practical Steps for Acquiring Cross-Cultural Negotiation Skills*, 70 TEX. B.J. 590, 591 (July 2007).

Instrumental

Some clients (and lawyers) see the world from a primarily instrumental standpoint. They perceive themselves to be actors capable of choosing causes to produce effects and influence outcomes. These clients think and act with confidence that actions produce predictable results. When clients operate from an instrumental standpoint, they consider what results their conduct will produce.

Lawyers are typically familiar with instrumental thinking. As professionals providing legal services, lawyers expect their actions and the actions of their clients to produce or at least influence results. On the other hand, lawyers work within complex systems in which the interests of their clients often conflict with the interests of others. Lawyers appreciate the limitations of instrumental actions, that they do not always produce the desired results.

Instrumental-thinking clients may not appreciate the limitations on instrumental thinking, especially when those clients are unfamiliar with the professional culture and competing interests through which lawyers address legal matters. In cross-cultural consultations, clients may expect a degree of certainty that the lawyer knows does not exist. Cross-cultural clients may exaggerate the lawyer's power to influence outcomes through instrumental actions. They may think that the lawyer can do, or that the client can do with the lawyer's help, more than the lawyer knows that they can confidently predict and accomplish.

Lawyers can recognize clients who think in overtly instrumental fashion. Statements from instrumental clients may include, "So, are you saying that if I do this, then that will happen?" and "Can you assure me that we will see that result?" The value of legal advice to an instrumental thinker tends to depend on the lawyer's ability to comprehend the critical context and predict the result. Instrumental thinking depends on both knowledge of the circumstance and experienced judgment as to outcomes and results.

Lawyers who recognize when their clients are using instrumental thinking can adapt advice to take account of the clients' reasoning. Lawyers may certainly help the client evaluate and predict the outcome of various courses of action. On the other hand, lawyers might also appropriately caution clients about the reliability of purely instrumental thinking and suggest instead considering the character of their actions and their fitness to the involved persons and circumstances. Consider an example.

"Well, I'm not so sure that you can be that confident about what you are proposing," the lawyer cautioned. The client had just recounted several unexpected reversals of fortune while at the same time expressing great confidence in the course on which the client was about to embark. "Have you thought about how she might respond when she gets the notice of hearing?" the lawyer asked.

The client was only momentarily taken aback before answering, "Of course. There's only one thing that she can do. And you'll make her do that." The lawyer saw the contrary that the client's opposing party had done the opposite of what the client expected at every opportunity that the opposing party had to choose and act. The lawyer suspected that the client had told the lawyer only a small portion of the relevant considerations and that the lawyer would have no more success than the client had in changing the outcome.

The lawyer asked the client again, "Is that what happened last time? How do you think your action made her feel? Why did the court take her side?" For the first time, the client was silent—indeed stumped. The lawyer had finally been able to show the client that the problem might not be with the court or opposing party but with the client's way of thinking about them.

"Well, I'm just doing what makes the most sense," the client finally ventured but this time with a lot less confidence. Now it was the lawyer's turn to speak with confidence. The lawyer and client spent the balance of the consultation working out a plan that, though instrumental in part, also had a balance of therapeutic, moral, and probabilistic considerations. The client left a lot less confident in the outcome but strangely more confident in the *outlook*.

Pragmatic

Instrumental thinking can be powerful, particularly when combined with pragmatic judgments about the client's capabilities and resources within the given circumstance. Pragmatic clients reason less about right and wrong, probabilities, and other remote considerations. They act more on the basis of immediate capabilities with less concern for long-term planning and effects. Consider another example.

"Let's take stock of what you have at hand," the lawyer finally suggested to the client after a rambling consultation that had produced no achievable plan. The disabled client and her mother lived unhappily in a rental property beset by drug dealers and prostitutes. The client had repeatedly challenged the landlord in court over the client's right to quiet enjoyment of the premises— and lost for the third time. This time, though, the court had imposed costs crippling the client's finances.

The client had brought along the appeal forms. She had been asking the lawyer about transcript orders and costs for an appeal that the client was adamant about pursuing but in which the lawyer saw little hope. "How will you pay those appeal costs?" the lawyer asked. The client finally stopped, admitting that the court had already refused a fee waiver. The lawyer and client finally turned to some simple options that would improve the client's housing situation.

To improve probabilistic, moral, and instrumental thinking, lawyers can help clients also think pragmatically, recognizing their practical abilities within their resource limitations. Lawyers who recognize when their clients are not exercising pragmatic reasoning and are struggling as a consequence may usefully pose pragmatic questions. Pragmatism can have considerable value to clients who face severe resource constraints. On the other hand, overly pragmatic judgments may produce even greater uncertainty than judgments made with some consideration given to general standards and for long-term predictable results. Lawyers do well to balance the pragmatic with the principled and to help their clients do the same, when clients are exercising instrumental thinking.

These reference systems are just a few of many reference systems that clients may use in thinking about and evaluating their legal matters. The challenge for a lawyer serving a cross-cultural client is to recognize the variety in reference systems, discern the client's commitments and preferences, and then help the client draw on the strengths and remediate the weaknesses of those preferences.

Reflections

Consider the following reflections on the above framework for supporting a cross-cultural client's worldview or reference system. Add these reflections to your journal. Find an acquaintance with whom to discuss these questions, or organize a group discussion, to broaden and enrich your view:

1. Discern your own personal worldview or perspective by ranking your top three reference points in order among (a) therapeutic, (b) providential, (c) probabilistic, (d) moral, (e) instrumental, and (f) pragmatic. What experiences caused you to adopt those perspectives?

2. How well or poorly have your perspectives served you in different situations? Do you alternate perspectives in different relationships or communities? If given the opportunity to adopt a fresh worldview or perspective, which one would you choose? Explain why. Which worldview would you adopt for a time of special challenge? Which worldview gives you the greatest satisfaction?

3. Does your personal perspective differ from your professional perspective? How did your professional perspective form? Who or what most influenced it? Which worldview do you first assume when working with a new client?

4. Think of an immediate family member whose worldview or perspective you know well. Identify one or two of the following as that family member's dominant perspective: (a) therapeutic, (b) providential, (c) probabilistic, (d) moral, (e) instrumental, or (f) pragmatic. How does that family member express that perspective? What would a stranger first notice about that family member's words or outlook that would disclose that family member's perspective?

5. Think of a phrase or statement you might hear from a client holding each of the following worldviews or perspectives: (a) therapeutic, (b) providential, (c) probabilistic, (d) moral, (e) instrumental, and (f) pragmatic. Now think of a phrase that you might use or statement that you might make in helping a client holding each of those worldviews to draw on it. Now think of a phrase or statement you would *not* make to a client holding each perspective.

6. For each of the following perspectives, identify a strength and weakness: (a) therapeutic, (b) providential, (c) probabilistic, (d) moral, (e) instrumental, and (f) pragmatic. How could the strength help the client facing a serious legal challenge? How could the weakness harm the client in the same situation? What perspective would you recommend the client consider to remediate the weakness?

Chapter 10

Resourceful

"Could someone else help me, please?"

Resources

She needed the job, but she was no longer sure that she needed *this* job. The young legal assistant had been delighted to join the small firm's office a year earlier. She had always wanted something to do with law and justice, a desire that she traced to the fact that her minority community seemed to have so little of it. Her first year at the firm had been one of substantial growth. She had learned a ton, she felt, while her finances, housing, transportation, and just about everything else had improved with the modest but steady income that the job provided. Months earlier, she had even begun to dream of going to law school, which recently had begun to feel to be solidly within her reach as she continued finishing one by one her night courses at community college.

She had just one problem. From nearly her first day on the job, she had noticed that the firm's lawyers and staff had been steering certain clients away from her, clients whose routine paperwork she would have readily handled just as she did for the firm's other clients. Barely more than a month into the job, she had learned the reason: those clients were asking for *white* help or at least to avoid *black* help.

At first, either the requests had not been so obvious or she had misunderstood their source. At first, she had attributed the requests to clients asking for someone *more experienced* than she was. The clients, she assumed, had not seen her in the office before and, when first meeting her, had taken her unfamiliarity to mean that she was *new* and perhaps therefore not so *skilled.* Some of the clients had sort of looked her up and down, and on a couple of those occasions she had been pretty sure what was going on, but she had just looked past it in part because she felt that she was still gaining her employer's trust. She also knew that the legal matters that clients were bringing to the firm were in most cases very personal and important, so for a long while she was just willing to ignore it.

She was not naïve. She knew all about prejudice. Her minority community and the neighboring majority community were about as segregated as one could find anywhere in the region. The communities had also had their conflict history and tensions. That conflict had been one of the reasons, though, that she had so appreciated and even celebrated this law firm job. She thought a lot of her employers for their having hired her. Yet as she gained skill and confidence, and saw that her work and habits were as good as or better than anyone else in the firm, she was less and less sure that she should keep letting these reassignments pass. In fact, she could see them interfering with her work and reputation.

Then one day it all blew up, those months and months of ignoring the obvious while stuffing those feelings down. A new client with a matter that she would have handled easily in her routine gathering of information and completing paperwork, had taken one look at her and without even taking her eyes off of her told the firm's managing partner behind her, "Could someone else help me, please?" Looking sheepishly at the young legal assistant, the lawyer had politely complied. As the two of them left the office, the young legal assistant heard the client use a racial slur in telling the lawyer that she did not want anyone of that race working on the client's matter.

Late that night, the legal assistant found what she had researched online through her anger and tears since the moment she had gotten home, which was clear authority that employers violate anti-discrimination laws when complying with client or customer racially discriminatory requests. She needed a job, just not *that* job.

Resource Expectations

Addressing legal issues requires resources. A client's money, time, health, vocation, transportation, flexibility of schedule, legal status, social support, and other resources can all contribute to how successfully the client addresses the client's legal matter with a lawyer's help. Abundant resources tend to make addressing a legal matter easier. Limited resources can make it harder. Severe resource limitations can make it impossible or require alternative plans. In any one matter, the presence or absence of a single specific resource, like legal status, can make all the difference to the client's success.

Lawyers in their standard practice may serve clients who have relatively uniform resources, whether abundant or limited. Lawyers fairly assume certain client resources within certain client populations and settings. Lawyers doing estate-planning work tend to have clients with financial resources, although the clients may not have time or good health. Lawyers handling Social Security-disability appeals tend to have clients with fewer financial resources. The clients will not have health or work, although they will likely have time and flexibility of schedule. Lawyers doing immigration work serve clients who lack legal status as a resource, although the clients may have money, vocation, transportation, family and social support, and other resources.

The relative uniformity of client resources within certain populations can mask for a lawyer the significance that those resources have to the soundness of the lawyer's advice. Given a standard set of client resources, a lawyer gives advice that accounts for and draws on those resources. The lawyer need not adjust advice significantly from client to client when client resources are relatively uniform. Individual resources can differ from client to client within client populations but even more so across client populations distinguished by region, socioeconomic

157

status, and other demographics including education, age, sex, race or ethnicity, and disability.

Adjusting Advice

When lawyers deal with clients of diverse socioeconomic and cultural backgrounds, they should consider differences in resources. Clients of diverse socioeconomic and cultural backgrounds may have different available resources, when contrasted with the population that a lawyer usually serves. Those differences may require the lawyer to alter the lawyer's standard advice to ensure that the client can achieve the consultation goal. Giving advice that a cross-cultural client cannot use because the client lacks necessary resources shows insensitivity to the client's circumstances. For effective cross-cultural service, lawyers should ensure that they understand the resources on which the usefulness of their advice depends. A lawyer should then ensure that the cross-cultural client has those resources.

Avoid assuming that resources exist or do not exist. Especially avoid blaming cross-cultural clients when their failure to follow a plan is due to lack of resources. Clients vary in their willingness and ability to communicate their resource limitations. Be sensitive not only to your client's available resources but to your client's willingness and ability to articulate them. Be aware of how your resources differ from those your cross-cultural clients possess and how that disparity may change your perspective or influence your advice. Consider ways in which you can help your cross-cultural clients draw on their available resources. Be ready to recognize, inventory, and draw on a cross-cultural client's particular resource strengths. Clients completely without material resources may yet possess significant character resources. Consider an example.

The lawyer and Hispanic-Latino client met in a cultural center familiar to the client. The lawyer had just explained the client's worker's compensation rights. The client knew that medical care and wage loss were the client's legal rights. Yet an awkward pause ensued when the lawyer gave the client a list of worker's compensation lawyers who would help the client on contingency-fee basis with an initial free consultation. The lawyer suspected what the pause meant. "I know a lawyer who is located on the bus line a few blocks away," the lawyer resumed, then adding, "His legal assistant speaks Spanish." The lawyer had already learned that the client lived just down the block and had walked to the cultural center. The client spoke just enough English to relate his legal issue with a little help from the cultural center's translator, who had attended the consultation just in case.

The lawyer watched the client brighten but still hesitate. "Would you like me to make you an appointment right now?" the lawyer asked, pulling a cell phone from a pocket and starting to look up and dial the number. The client nodded. "What is your best time and day?" the lawyer asked as he wrote out the bus line, bus stop, lawyer's name, firm name, and office address. The client and translator chatted in Spanish while the lawyer confirmed the appointment over the cell phone.

> "Decades of statistical research document the racial disparities inherent in the system:
>
> • African-Americans are incarcerated at nearly six times the rate of whites.
>
> • African-American males have a 32% chance of serving time in prison at some point in their lives; Hispanic males have a 17% chance, and Caucasian males have a 6% chance.
>
> • In 2000, African-Americans were 13% of the resident population but represented 44% of all convicted federal offenders.
>
> • In 2008, 10.4% African-American males aged 25–29 were in prison or jail, as were 3.8% Hispanic and1.6% Caucasian males in the same age group." American Bar Association, *Building Community Trust: Improving Cross-cultural Communication in the Criminal Justice System* 2-3 (June 2010) (footnotes omitted).

Resource Framework

As is true for cross-cultural client communication, cognition, and reference, a framework can help a lawyer discern cross-cultural client resource differences. As in the case of communication, cognition, and reference, the resource framework offered below will use several measures including (a) finances, (b) housing, (c) transportation, (d) legal status, and (e) time. Consider each measure briefly before further discussion below.

Resources certainly include money and basic necessities that money buys like food. The client who lacks the fees to pay for a necessary filing will need other advice regarding available fee waivers. The client who must be at a soup kitchen to eat or in a food line at a specific time to take a meal home to children may be unable to do other activities that the lawyer's advice requires. A lawyer's planning should account for a cross-cultural client's limited finances. Resources also include housing both for its physical accommodation and for its legal sense of an official address. Homelessness itself can give rise to legal issues like disorderly conduct, vagrancy, nuisance, and trespass. The homeless client who has no address may not be able to receive necessary mail, establish residence for public rights or benefits, or give a necessary official address. A lawyer's advice should account for a cross-cultural client's housing and residence.

Transportation is another resource. Law involves places like offices, courthouses, jails, probation offices, and administrative agencies. Access to justice often requires getting physically to those places. Unavailable transportation can alone turn otherwise-sound legal advice into wasted effort, when the advice fails to account for that resource limitation. Lawyers should adjust advice to account for a cross-cultural client's transportation issues. Resources can also mean a recognized legal status. A cross-cultural client who has an undocumented legal status may not be willing or able to follow a lawyer's advice, especially if the advice entails recourse to law enforcement, courthouses, or other government agencies. Undocumented legal status can interfere directly with employment, public benefits, and other opportunities and rights. It can also change the way in which a client and opposing party evaluate relative rights.

Finally, resources can also mean time including flexibility of schedule and a calendar or other means by which to keep a schedule. Clients experience law as a matter of time involving limitations periods, due dates, hearing dates, waiting periods, and delays. Now consider each of these five measures in detail.

Finances

The financial resources clients have to pay for legal and law-related services obviously vary. Yet legal fees aside, even when clients have appointed lawyers or pro bono lawyers, some clients will not have the money or finances for court filing fees, copies, service fees, and other expenses necessary to advancing the representation. Direct lack of income may not be the problem for many clients. Even clients who are not able to earn income will often be receiving or eligible to receive public support. Rather, the financial resource limitation is that clients can lack discretionary funds to devote to legal matters. A fee as small as $2 or $5 can be an impediment to obtaining legal service when 70% of the client's $550 per month income goes to housing and the rest the client must devote to food, personal items, and medical care.

Be sensitive to financial-resource disparities. Carefully consider the costs of each action you propose to a client who lacks discretionary income. Be sure to help clients understand even small costs of representation. Help clients plan for meeting those costs. Your help may be as simple as directing the client to a legal assistance center where the client can complete a form for a fee waiver. Do not assume on the basis of clothing or other appearances that funds are available to a client. The sudden disruption of employment, family, and other relationships can make finances unavailable to those who usually have access to them. Consider an example.

"Absolutely, there is help available," the lawyer reassured the client in the domestic-violence shelter, adding, "Just go to the Legal Assistance Center on the fifth floor of the Courthouse, and the staff will help you fill out the court papers."

The client was decently dressed and seemingly accustomed to middle-class income. The lawyer had learned, though, that she was living with her infant son in the homeless mission needing help with a family-law matter. The lawyer explained the forms the client would need to complete and then wrote instructions for the client including to ask for a fee waiver.

"Be sure to take a couple of dollars, though," the lawyer added, concluding, "The only cost they do not waive is for making copies of the papers, and that alone is going to be at least a couple dollars." The client thanked the lawyer, adding that she could get a couple of dollars from her friends at the mission.

A cross-cultural client's limited finances may mean that the client has limited access to basic necessities. A client's challenges associated with obtaining necessities can also affect a lawyer's advice. Given available food pantry and soup kitchen programs, actual hunger may relatively infrequently be a direct impediment to a client's ability to follow legal advice. On the other hand, some clients must devote a disproportionate amount of their resources, including time and money, to obtaining food and making it consumable for themselves and their families. Bags of food may be available free at a church, community center, or government office. Yet the client may have to expend other resources such as time, money for public or private transportation, or social support arranging for child care, to obtain that food, preserve it, and prepare it for consumption. Understand and respect those demands upon a client's time and other resources that may come from having limited money. Look for opportunities to help those clients with copying, mailing, service of process, and other legal tasks that other clients might easily accomplish with greater financial resources. Consider another example.

"I only have a couple of minutes to talk with you before I go to work, so I hope we can get right to the point," the client hurriedly explained as she pulled court papers from her cloth shopping bag. The lawyer had grown accustomed to these hurried consultations with the mentally disabled client. The lawyer knew that the client's only income was from cleaning rooms each afternoon at a boarding house just down the urban street. The client received extra food for cleanup she did at a soup kitchen. The client's meager financial earnings, coupled with retirement benefits her live-in mother received, were just enough to pay utilities and taxes on the run-down home they owned.

From the client's anemic and unkempt appearance, those finances were not enough to keep her well-fed, cared-for, or clothed. "Look, are you going to be here next week?" the client asked, looking at the clock on the wall, "I just really have got to get going to my job." The lawyer reassured the client that she could see him again next week, and off she went.

> "The juxtaposition of an overwhelmingly Caucasian criminal justice infrastructure with the low socio-economic profile and varied cultural backgrounds of those brought before the criminal justice system—whether as victims, witnesses, defendants, or otherwise—has combined with other factors to generate increasing skepticism from many communities about the integrity and reliability of the criminal justice system. Racial disparities in prosecution and incarceration rates, high profile exonerations, and the disproportionate impact of poverty on communities of color with high crime rates combine to fuel community distrust of the criminal justice system and its actors. Community perceptions of judicial and prosecutorial bias contribute to this skepticism and distrust. Significantly under-funded public defense programs in many jurisdictions limit the time, tools, and training available to defenders to provide adequate representation of clients, further exacerbating community perceptions about the integrity and fairness of the criminal justice system." American Bar Association, *Building Community Trust: Improving Cross-cultural Communication in the Criminal Justice System* 3 (June 2010) (footnotes omitted).

Housing

Lawyers advising cross-cultural clients may need to consider the client's housing situation when shaping advice. Housing arrangements (including heat, hot water, and available restroom) can vary more widely among cross-cultural clients than a lawyer serving a homogenous population might expect. Some clients may have been homeless for an extended time. Others may have recently lost permanent housing because of sudden changes in job or relationships and may have only temporary shelter. Others may move frequently among temporary quarters.

Housing can impact legal advice. Certainly, unstable housing can require that the client devote disproportionate time and other resources to securing, preserving, or improving it, detracting from the client's ability to attend to the legal matter. Respect those demands and limitations when allocating tasks between lawyer and client on a legal matter. The absence of stable housing can also directly affect a lawyer's legal advice and the client's ability to benefit from it. Establishing a client's residence may be necessary or helpful for divorce, child custody, parenting time, compliance with family-law orders, enforcement of family-law orders, compliance with terms of sentence or probation, compliance with registration schemes, receipt of public benefits, and other legal matters.

The absence of a reliable permanent address that the client can list and where the client can securely receive mail, can also affect a lawyer's legal advice and the client's ability to benefit from it. Probation offices, friend-of-court offices, court clerks, bankruptcy clerks, welfare offices, employers, unemployment offices, insurers, and others may require a client address for the client to have access to associated rights and benefits. The client's lawyer may well need an address to continue the representation. Addresses and contact information typically depend on stable housing. Courts and administrative agencies depend on having a party's current address. Lawyers, too, need a way to reach a client. When a client's unstable housing does not permit it, explore options with the client such as using a relative's or private social-service nonprofit's address.

Keep in mind that stable housing is not always related to socioeconomic status. Separations, domestic violence, arrests, job loss, and other unanticipated events can quickly change a client's housing resources. Housing issues can in several respects affect a client's willingness to disclose information and ability to accomplish legal tasks and meet legal requirements. Be prepared to help clients confirm or establish a reliable mailing address. Relatives may agree to accept a client's mail. The client may be able to obtain a post-office box. A homeless shelter or other local organization serving the underprivileged may have a mail service. Consider an example.

"Alright, then, what address shall we use for the court filing?" the lawyer asked the 40-year-old cross-cultural client with the bright but crooked smile and the painful history of severely violent domestic abuse. The client had just recovered from a fractured jaw at the hands of her estranged husband. She and the lawyer had been planning child and spousal-support matters around the restraining order that was in place as a result.

"Well," the client answered, "you know how to reach me at the shelter, and I will come see you here in any case." The lawyer knew why the client hesitated but also knew that both the client and lawyer needed her to have a reliable mailing address. The last time, the client had given the court her temporary address on the assurance that the court would keep it confidential from her estranged husband. The court had mistakenly disclosed her temporary address in an exchange of paperwork with her husband. Her fractured jaw was the result.

The lawyer interjected, "What if we use your sister's address for the court?" Lawyer and client discussed the options, finally agreeing that the client's sister was the most reliable custodian for her mail. The lawyer saw the client again a few weeks later, confirming that the arrangement had worked out.

Transportation

Lawyers advising cross-cultural clients may need to consider the client's available transportation more often than in the usual consultation. Transportation can vary more widely in cross-cultural consultations than the lawyer may expect in the lawyer's usual client population. Availability of a current driver's license, access to a registered and insured vehicle, and knowledge of locations and routes may all differ. Some clients may have no transportation or only unreliable transportation.

Whether the client has transportation available can affect a lawyer's legal advice. Clients who lack transportation or reliable transportation may find it difficult or impossible to make court or administrative-agency appearances. Transportation can affect a client's ability to obtain forms and signatures, copy and mail documents, secure witnesses, and perform other tasks that other clients would routinely perform in connection with their legal matters.

For clients who have limited transportation resources, clearly articulate the transportation requirements. Ensure that the client understands and can meet those requirements. Where the client lacks transportation interfering with the client's ability to follow your advice, help the client explore and confirm alternative plans. Keep in mind that some courts and agencies will permit video or telephone appearances, or written submissions in lieu of appearances. Impress on the client the need to notify the court or agency when unable to attend. Advise the client regarding the consequences of a failure to appear so that the client appreciates why transportation is necessary. Be prepared to modify your communications with courts and agencies to indicate that a transportation-limited client may be unable to attend. If necessary, request waiver of appearance and hearing.

Do not leave clients without alternative plans for notice to the court or agency, or alternative means of appearing. The hazards of doing so include that the client may simply ignore the legal matter at greater peril, when the legal system appears to impose an impossible requirement. When you are able, offer to perform or ask your office staff to perform tasks that other clients would perform on their own making use of better transportation. Consider an example.

Nearing the end of the lawyer's consultation, the grizzled, mentally disabled Vietnam veteran finally understood the administrative appeal procedure he would need to pursue to gain access once again to the medical clinic where he had threatened the staff. The lawyer was already familiar with the client's post-traumatic stress disorder typically expressed in rage. The client had disclosed that the client had committed a series of stupidly violent acts against individuals—social service workers, family members, employers—who had been trying to help the client. The problem remained, though, that the client had no way to get to the state capitol where the agency would hold the administrative hearing for the client to regain his medical-access rights. "See this toll-free number on the back of the form," the lawyer explained. "Calling that number today will enable you to attend the hearing by telephone. Would that help?" the lawyer offered.

The client grunted assent. The lawyer then offered to make the call. The administrative law judge's clerk confirmed for the lawyer that she had marked the hearing down to receive the veteran's toll-free call. The lawyer read the number back to the clerk as he wrote it on the pad for the veteran, along with the day, date, and time of the hearing.

Legal Status

Lawyers advising cross-cultural clients may need to consider the client's legal status more often than in the usual consultation. Legal status can vary more often in cross-cultural consultations than the lawyer may expect in the lawyer's usual client population. The cross-cultural client may have no documented status or may have only a resident-alien, temporary, or otherwise-limited status. Resident-alien, temporary, limited, or undocumented status can significantly affect a client's legal rights and resources, and ability to follow a lawyer's advice. Legal status goes beyond immigration-law concerns. Some clients may have a criminal record that affects their ability to obtain housing or employment, or that carries with it other consequences collateral to the conviction.

In important respects, legal status is a resource. Legal status can have a significant impact on advice. A lawyer may help a client plan for deportation by preparing or advising a limited power of attorney for guardianship of minor, U.S.-citizen children. Even where legal status is not relevant to the legal rights and duties of a client, the client may misperceive that legal status does have an effect. Be prepared to reassure resident-alien or undocumented clients when their status does not affect their ability to hold property, enforce contracts, and access the courts. When planning legal matters with cross-cultural clients, be

167

sensitive to potential legal-status issues. Your direct questions regarding the client's legal status may or may not be appropriate. When legal-status questions may be affecting the client's evaluation of options, but the client appears unwilling to disclose the client's legal status, explain how involved courts or agencies will treat legal-status issues. Consider an example.

To the lawyer, the cross-cultural client's course seemed convenient and clear. "The district court's small-claims division does not require a lawyer," the lawyer explained, waiting for the translator to finish before adding, "It does not even allow lawyers. You can handle it just fine." Still, the client appeared hesitant to take the small-claims forms that the lawyer was offering.

The lawyer had already filled out the form and explained what to expect when the client appeared for the small-claims hearing. They had already confirmed that the client would appear with a translator. Gross injustice would result if the client did not pursue a small claim. The claim was precisely why the client had sought the lawyer's advice.

Only then did it occur to the lawyer. "Just last week I heard Judge Martinez explain to a group of law students that the district court has no referral system or other connection with immigration officials," the lawyer ventured, being sure to pause over the judge's Hispanic-Latino surname. "The judge felt that the district court should be a safe place for any non-violent person for whom no arrest warrant is in place to settle basic rights."

The client nodded in apparent relief, took the forms, and thanked the lawyer in Spanish. Lawyer and client rose and shook hands, and the client departed. After the client left, the lawyer and translator simply looked at one another and smiled until the translator added, "That Judge Martinez, he's a good one."

"Disproportionality in the criminal justice system exists when the proportion of a racial or ethnic group within the control of the system is greater than the proportion of such groups in the general population. For example, African-Americans make up 12% of the U.S. population, but account for approximately 40% of all arrests, 50% of the prison population, and 50% of the inmates on death row. Racial disparity also occurs when there is a significantly larger percentage of members of a minority group involved in a part of the criminal justice system than Caucasians. For example, more than 4.6% of all African-American adult males are in jail or in prison, compared with .07% of all Caucasian adult males; African Americans are 13.4 times as likely as Caucasians to be arrested on drug charges, even though Caucasians use drugs at five times the rate.

"Racial disparity in the criminal justice system refers to the dissimilar treatment of similarly situated people based on race. The causes of such disparity are varied and can include law enforcement emphasis on particular communities, legislative policies, and/or decision-making by criminal justice practitioners who exercise broad discretion in the justice process at one or more stages in the system. In some instances this may involve overt racial bias; while in others, it may reflect the influence of factors that are only indirectly associated with race. Moreover, in some cases disparity results from unguarded, individual- or institution-level decisions that are race-based." American Bar Association, *Building Community Trust: Improving Cross-cultural Communication in the Criminal Justice System* 54-55 (June 2010) (footnotes omitted).

Time

Professional culture recognizes some variation in time norms. Some clients are routinely 15 minutes early for every appointment, considering it disrespectful to be as little as one minute late. Other clients are routinely 5 to 15 minutes late, considering it disrespectful to be as little as 5 minutes early. Respectfully on time, respectfully late, and fashionably late are conventions lawyers recognize, within relatively limited time constraints.

Yet time is metaphor. The way that clients conceptualize and use time can vary, especially in cross-cultural consultations. Lawyers serving a single relatively homogenous client population may give little thought to how diverse clients conceptualize and make use of time. Indeed, the phrase to *make use* of time presumes that time is a sort of commodity, when culture influences even that presumption.

Some cultures treat time as monochromic, assigning dates and times to events on points along a linear time continuum from past into the future while accepting that all members of the community share the same time continuum. A lawyer's professional culture certainly treats time in that monochromic, linear, and shared manner. Other cultures treat time as polychromic, placing past and anticipated future events in indeterminate individual arrays, vistas, or webs of experience, rather than in determinate points on a monochromic continuum. Members of those cultures do not necessarily connect their time constructs to the constructs of others. While professional culture tends to see time one way, as monochromic, clients influenced by other cultural time norms may see time in another way, as polychromic.

Culturally influenced time orientation can be a source for inappropriately negative pathological conceptualizations. Lawyers should not misunderstand differing time norms to indicate client disrespect or carelessness. The caution not to think less of a cross-cultural client who fails to make a scheduled event is especially apt given other potential demands and constraints that such clients may face. Unpredictable and inflexible events of importance come up for clients, just as they do for lawyers. Client schedules change. Scheduled dates may conflict with other inflexible client schedules, such as probation or parole appointments, substance-abuse counseling sessions or testing ("drops"), and parenting-time pick-up or drop-off. Clients needing food, temporary shelter, or other social services may have to be at a certain place at a certain time for those services. Charitable work-for-food and occupational rehabilitation programs can impose other time and schedule constraints.

These events may keep a client from making appointments for the client's legal matter. Lawyers should be aware that cross-cultural clients can have inflexible schedules and conflicts. Help clients plan accordingly. Clients may vary in their schedule demands, their ability to alter schedules to address legal issues, and their ability to maintain a calendar or other system by which to keep a schedule. Again, ensure that the cross-cultural client understands the consequence of missing scheduled appearances in offices or court, or at administrative agencies. One way of ensuring that cross-cultural clients have consistent access to counsel is to make a consistent time available for them every month or week. If the lawyer remains consistently available, then the client will have a reliable way of reaching the lawyer when the client is able and in need. Consider a brief example.

The client at the cultural center had asked the lawyer if she could see him the following week at the same time. "I'll be here," the lawyer replied, adding, "I hope you can make it." The client asked the lawyer to confirm the day and time. "It's every Thursday afternoon, just like today," the lawyer replied, adding, "Remember that if you can't see me here, you can always see the lawyers at the mission Wednesday afternoon."

Reflections

Consider the following reflections on the above framework for recognizing and respecting a cross-cultural client's resources and resource limitations. Add these reflections to your journal. Find an acquaintance with whom to discuss these questions, or organize a group discussion, to broaden and enrich your view:

1. Recall an instance when you lacked one of the following resources, in a way that interfered with your educational, vocational, financial, or legal responsibilities: (a) finances; (b) housing; (c) transportation; (d) legal status; and (e) time. What was the consequence to you for not having that resource? How did you minimize the consequence?

2. For each of the following resources, identify a family member, friend, or acquaintance who lacks that resource: (a) finances; (b) housing; (c) transportation; (d) legal status; and (e) time. Describe the challenges that the resource's absence presents for the person you identified.

3. Rate as *greater than*, *equal to*, or *less than* each of the following resources you have available to you, relative to the general population of the community in which you live: (a) finances; (b) housing; (c) transportation; (d) legal status; and (e) time. In which measure do you have the greatest resource advantage over others in your community? In which measure do

you have the greatest disadvantage contrasted to others in your community?

4. For each of the following resources, estimate the percentage of the population of the community in which you live that has a substantial lack of that resource affecting the person's ability to lead a normal life: (a) finances; (b) housing; (c) transportation; (d) legal status; and (e) time. What other substantial resource limitations do individuals face in your community (education, health care, physical security, clean environment, etc.)?

5. Rate as *greater than*, *equal to*, or *less than* each of the following resources you have available to you, relative to the client population you serve or plan to serve: (a) finances; (b) housing; (c) transportation; (d) legal status; and (e) time. In which measure do you have the greatest resource advantage over your clients or anticipated clients?

6. For each of the following resources, identify a way in which its absence or limitation on the part of the client may affect your legal advice to that client: (a) finances; (b) housing; (c) transportation; (d) legal status; and (e) time. How would you change your advice to remediate the absence of that resource?

Chapter 11

Relational

"I'm not talking about *you!*"

Relationship Expectations

The majority-ethnicity client had poured her heart out to the lawyer about the challenges that she had faced in a difficult domestic relationship with a man who just happened to share the lawyer's minority ethnicity. The client had failed to realize until the end of her ramblings that she had made several negative references to the man's ethnicity, that very ethnicity that the lawyer coincidentally shared with the client's adversary. The lawyer had listened patiently without interrupting the client, although of course the lawyer had silently noted the unfortunate ethnic references. The references could, after all, have been important clues to addressing the client's legal issues in her difficult cross-cultural relationship.

Indeed, the lawyer had already discerned in the client's story probable differences in the ways that the client and her adversary had expected to conduct the relationship. The client had plainly not seen those different expectations, even though her story made them apparent. Instead, the client construed her relationship challenges as the man's *fault*, indeed attributing the relationship's breakdown to deep character *defects* in the man. The lawyer certainly recognized that the client's assessment could have been accurate. We all have defects. Yet the client's negative ethnic references, very like evident racial prejudice, at least suggested that other causes more within the client's control could have contributed to the difficulties in the relationship.

Just as the client ended her account, and the lawyer politely listening to the client returned to her mind's focus, the client finally made the connection. She for the first time noticed the lawyer's ethnicity. The lawyer's high reputation, supervisory role, and professional demeanor and dress might initially have hidden that realization from the client, just as the professional office setting may also have momentarily relieved the client from the burden of her prejudice. Whatever the cause, the client now realized not so much that she might have offended the lawyer but that she had something to correct.

"Of course, I'm not talking about *you*," the client offered in excuse for the racial bias that she had several times expressed when complaining about her adversary who shared her lawyer's ethnicity. The statement seemed to satisfy the client, confirming in the lawyer's mind the additional important data that the client lacked insight into the staining power of prejudice. The lawyer spent the next few minutes of the consultation gently coaxing the client toward recognizing how individuals can construct and conduct relationships differently depending on their practices and preferences, and that some of the difficulties she had faced may in part have been due to those different relationship expectations.

Relationship Differences

Lawyers in their standard practices develop standard forms of relationship with clients. Relationship forms may differ somewhat across legal fields. Estate planners and family-law lawyers may in their representation develop greater family context and, in doing so, become closer to clients than business or personal-injury lawyers. Yet lawyers generally have a relatively uniform set of expectations for the client relationship. Those usual expectations tend to include that the representation involves a transaction—a bargained-for service in which the client expects the lawyer to convey something of value. Lawyers tend to base the professional relationship on the service's value and expect clients to do the same. After all, clients pay for most service. They should receive a valuable service in return.

The usual expectations also tend to include that the lawyer is the expert and the client the non-expert. This second expectation is a corollary of the first expectation. If the relationship depends on the transaction, and the transaction involves a conveyance of valued service, then the lawyer should be expert in that service, and the client, needing the service, should be a relative non-expert. Other relationship forms exist beyond these sensible assumptions. Some lawyers may not recognize other appropriate forms of professional relationship. Some lawyers may serve a sufficiently homogenous client population that they have little need and opportunity to develop appropriate variety in professional relationships.

Lawyers who serve cross-cultural clients should avoid assuming that the usual way in which they conceive of the professional relationship will best serve all clients. Some clients, and especially cross-cultural clients, may benefit more by a different form of appropriate professional relationship. Be sensitive not only to your client's need for services but to your client's need for certain forms of professional relationship. Here, too, self-knowledge is an important step toward intercultural competence. Be aware of how you conceive of and treat the professional relationship. Recognize that your cross-cultural client may have, desire, or benefit from an alternative conception. Consider ways in which you can appropriately alter your standard treatment of the relationship in order to better serve unique or unusual client needs.

"As the use of mediation increases, mediators are more likely to be involved in cross-cultural mediation. Even the most skilled and experienced mediator will face new challenges in cross-cultural mediation. Although only a handful of mediators have the opportunity to mediate cross-border business disputes or international political conflicts, domestic mediators are increasingly likely to be involved in disputes between people who represent distinctly different ethnic, racial, or national origin cultures. ...

"How extreme and important can cultural differences be? When we encounter people from different cultures, their language and nonverbal communication may be different, and they can be very different in other fundamental ways that impact their behavior, view of life, values, the way they see and solve problems, and make decisions." John Barkai, *What's a Cross-Cultural Mediator to Do? A Low-Context Solution for a High-Context Problem*, 10 CARDOZO J. CONFLICT RES. 43, 43, 47 (2008) (footnotes omitted).

Relationship and Culture

Culture influences relationship. A useful way to think about cultural differences in relationship forms is that individuals of different cultures form relationships along various spectrums. In any one culture, individuals may desire to form relationship at the cultural standard point along these spectrums. Those spectrums can include individual to collective, where clients of different cultures think more or less about their individual interests and give greater or lesser regard for family, community, or other collective interests. Some cultures are highly individualistic, while others are highly collective, and still others fall in between. A client from a highly individualistic culture may not desire advice about collective interests, while a client from a highly collective culture may desire that advice and eschew advice about individual interests.

Those spectrums can also include independent to interdependent to dependent. Clients may think and act independently, taking the lawyer's advice as just that, something to consider but take or leave for what the client independently judges the advice to be worth. Alternatively, clients may think dependently, expecting the lawyer to choose and act on their behalf with the client's authority but without the client making judgments. In between these two ends of the spectrum, a client may expect interdependent action where lawyer and client each act only when involving the other.

Those spectrums can also include competing to sharing. The client may treat the lawyer as an adversary against whom the client must compete, whether for fees or time or the like. The client may instead treat the lawyer as a co-participant sharing in the client's matter. Clients can also choose relationship forms from authoritarian to egalitarian and along other spectrums.

Client relationship expectations extend beyond the professional relationship to relationship with others. One client may act as a loner, eschew offers of help, hoard resources, and demand rights and equal treatment from others. Another client may act like an old friend, welcome social and other support, give away personal assets, and readily submit to the superior rights and authority of others. These and other behaviors may have much to do with the way the client anticipates and constructs relationships. The best practice is not to simply know thyself, the client with whom one deals, and the client's matter. The best practice is also to know the relationship.

As in the case of communication, cognition, reference, and resource, a framework for relationship forms can help a lawyer recognize alternative forms. Once again, like the prior chapters, this chapter offers just five models, here for professional relationship. You can discern other relationship models from the above spectrums. The following five relationship models should give you a useful heuristic for recognizing other models. Consider the following five-part framework, completing the overall framework for discerning cross-cultural client norms.

"Culturally savvy associates ... become adept at client development across cultures. Many seasoned lawyers never bother to cultivate these skills. As our economy (and the resulting legal work) becomes more global, however, cross-cultural acumen will increasingly be prized.

"Learn to develop good rapport with people from different cultures. Opportunities to do this abound—whether through alumni groups, intercultural organizations or everyday life. ...

"Personal branding also impacts rainmaking success when building connections with people from other cultures. How you dress, talk, communicate with clients, and produce work product all contribute to your personal brand. ... [S]howcase attributes that strengthen your brand—especially those that make you more marketable in a global environment. For example, perhaps you speak—but rarely use—a foreign language. Polish your language skills and let clients and co-workers know about your proficiency.

"Culturally savvy associates are best positioned to rise in our global economy. Implement these strategies and watch your star rise." Janet H.

Moore, *The Culturally Savvy Associate: Top Three Tips for Moving Up in a Global Economy*, Law Practice (ABA 2010).

Transactional

As indicated above, one common conception of the professional relationship is as a transaction for services between independent selves. Some clients will expect that the lawyer treat the professional relationship as an exchange of a valued service for consideration of some kind—payment, a promise to pay, or good will, for example. Cross-cultural clients preferring transactional relationship may choose not to engage in any professional communication that to them appears to go beyond the information strictly necessary for the legal service. These clients may see behaviors, their own in particular but yours as well, as determined by underlying stable dispositions and strong will. These clients may in extreme cases even decline to disclose their name, address, or other identifying information.

Cross-cultural clients preferring transactional relationship may be especially reluctant to share the social context out of which their legal issue arose. Transactional relationship preserves emotional distance and privacy. Do not be surprised or offended if some cross-cultural clients essentially say, "It is none of your business." Avoid seeming to pry. When you have a need for certain information that seems to the client to be irrelevant and private, explain the need, and reassure the client that you are not prying. Lawyers should be sensitive to these clients' unwillingness to disclose personal, marriage, family, and other information that another client would exchange freely in more trusting or open professional relationships. Listen for words and watch for behaviors that signal the client's desire to restrict the relationship to purely transactional form.

Lawyers can provide meaningful legal service without getting to know the client in any larger or whole sense or inviting a different professional relationship. Privacy can be rare and precious especially for homeless clients or other clients who depend on social services. Think twice before making any public acknowledgment of a professional relationship. Let the client lead in choosing the relationship form. Consider an example.

The furtive cross-cultural client might have been a man or might have been a woman—not that it mattered, for the client was not willing even to share a name no less an address, employer, or other identifying information. When the lawyer just started to extend a gentle hand, the client deliberately looked away and tucked hands under the arms. The lawyer just nodded politely and motioned graciously toward the chair. The client looked intently at the folder and pen the lawyer had in his free hand, so the lawyer set it aside.

"Anything we talk about here is privileged," the lawyer reassured the client, "No one else will know unless you want them to know." With those and other reassurances, the client described in veiled terms an encounter with an unnamed employer that had resulted in job termination and some unpaid wages. The lawyer described the law also identifying the website where the client could make an online complaint. The client then simply rose and left with hardly a word of acknowledgment.

A couple of times the lawyer passed the same client on the street but, recalling the client's reticence, made and received no greeting or other acknowledgment. The client returned on one other occasion with a different legal matter exhibiting the same veiled conduct. Evidently, the lawyer's first transaction had satisfied the mysterious client.

Relational

The transactional model for professional relationship, though common, is not the only model or necessarily the best model for all clients. Some clients, and particularly cross-cultural clients who are unfamiliar with professional norms, may not be accustomed and may not desire to treat a person-to-person relationship in transactional terms. To a cross-cultural client unfamiliar with professional norms, transactional relationship can seem cold, uncaring, or even calculating and competitive. Cross-cultural clients may be accustomed to treating participants in any relationship including professional relationships as having inherent value. They may not distinguish professional relationship from personal relationship, family relationship, or friend relationship. They may look at all relationship as based on the intrinsic value of each participant, without regard to their productive capabilities.

Cross-cultural clients who think and behave relationally may feel that the consultation was worthwhile whether or not the lawyer provided a service having some positive effect on their legal situation. You may have been unsuccessful in influencing any positive change in their legal matter but still have an appreciative client. Lawyers should be aware that relational clients see the professional relationship in a larger sense, as having larger purposes and possibilities beyond the transaction or exchange. The consultation may have produced no discernible change in the client's legal matter this time, but it might with the next matter. Having a lawyer available has its own benefits, even if the lawyer cannot help every time.

Even when the lawyer is unable to help, the lawyer and client may nonetheless have enjoyed the time, or been inspired by or learned from one another. Clients model lawyer behavior. You may see a cross-cultural client several times, knowing that your consultation produced no change in the client's legal situation. Yet you may also discern that the client has drawn new confidence, cognitive skill, or administrative insight from your consultations. In cross-cultural consultations, be willing to treat the relational client as a person more so than a problem to solve. Take an appropriate level of interest in their humanity even while focusing on the legal matter at hand. Lawyers can provide meaningful legal service while also getting to know and appreciate clients in larger perspective. They can also provide meaningful service simply by acknowledging the client's circumstance and standing. Consider an example.

The older gentleman, fastidiously dressed and groomed, greeted the lawyer formally through the translator, who had herself assumed a much more formal posture than usual. The translator was trying to look regal, in due regard for the gentleman client.

The gentleman client began to speak with a pained expression as he related an old grievance against a former business partner nearly a decade ago. Still bearing that look of pained insult, he then moved into consecutive but separate stories of bureaucratic bungling, family problems, and employment issues. The lawyer tried a few times to interject some legal counsel, but it only momentarily slowed and distracted the client before he moved on to the next grievance. Just to ensure that the lawyer was not missing some important right or claim, the lawyer silently listed on a legal pad 10 different marginally legal issues the gentleman client's long story evoked. Yet the client rebuffed any effort on the lawyer's part to make their encounter transactional and consultative.

Gradually, the lawyer realized the gentleman client's motivation for seeking out the lawyer. When the client finally concluded 30 minutes of uninterrupted recitation of a litany of insults against the client, the lawyer simply said, "You are obviously a man of great faith, respect, and distinction." Here, the lawyer paused to ensure that the translator conveyed the communication with the seriousness and weight that the lawyer intended. The translator did so, the lawyer could tell from her formal posture still mimicking the regal posture of the gentleman client.

"I admire you for persevering with such courage and resolve through so difficult a life," the lawyer continued, adding, "I thank you for honoring me, your humble professional, with your gracious presence." For the first time the gentleman client smiled, looking like a great weight had been lifted from his shoulders. The lawyer waited for the client to ask what the lawyer was going to do for him, but instead, the client rose, bowed formally, extended his hand, and left in complete satisfaction, the lawyer shaking the client's hand in parting with all the formality that the lawyer could muster. Evidently, the lawyer thought, not every consultation involves a necessary transaction.

"There are compelling rationales for diversity and inclusion in the legal profession. In April 2010, the American Bar Association released its 'Next Steps' report, which focused on the following four rationales:

"(1) **Democracy.** Lawyers play a unique role in all spheres of life, including all branches of the United States government—a government of the people, by the people, and for the people. This democracy was designed as a representative government, though it has not always lived up to that high ideal. A broader base of citizen participation in governing and developing the rule of law is needed. Because lawyers contribute mightily to governance and development of the law, a legal profession that is diverse and inclusive is necessary to achieve the goals of a representative democracy.

"(2) **Business.** We live in a global world. The trend toward globalization will not reverse. Given the globalization of economies, business, customers, and cultures, we must increase the diversity of the American legal profession to mirror the global population it serves.

"(3) **Leadership.** This country has a love-hate relationship with lawyers. However, lawyers play a major role in politics on national, state, and local levels. Lawyers also have a great deal of power in private industry and elsewhere. These facts make it clear that lawyers are and will continue to be influential decision makers in this country.

"(4) **Demographics.** The United States Census reports that by 2042, the majority of citizens in this country will be people of color, as opposed to white Caucasians. Hispanics were reported as the largest minority group in the latest census, and their population exceeds that of black Americans by a few percentage points." Hon. Victoria A. Roberts & John R. Nussbaumer, *Progress Report on the SBM Pledge to Achieve Diversity and Inclusion*, 91/1 MICH. B.J. 20 (January 2012).

Expert

Cross-cultural clients can also vary in the degree to which they will respect and relies on a lawyer's expertise. Lawyers are generally the authority in professional relationships, even while deferring to and drawing on the higher authority of judges and other public officials. Lawyers seldom have difficulty exhibiting expertise to clients and fashioning professional relationship around that expertise. Yet lawyers may not always appreciate that clients, not lawyers, define the scope and responsibility of the lawyer's authority, and that cross-cultural clients may differ from the lawyer's expectation as to that scope and responsibility.

Clients may legitimately request, require, and demand that the lawyer exercise appropriate authority. The lawyer's exercise of authority may in the client's view be essential to maintaining order within the client's affairs. This vertical form of relationship, demanding that the lawyer authority take responsibility for the client subject, is in some communities and situations a sound and acceptable way of forming relationship. The professional relationship in such cases is less one involving a transaction than one in which the relationship is one of client subject invoking the responsibility of lawyer authority. Clients may also make appropriate claims on lawyers as instruments of public justice in the protection of communities and clients. The lawyer's oath not to turn away the poor and defenseless recognizes that dependent form of relationship. Not every professional relationship need be a transaction. Lawyers can take the role of protector.

These authority and protector roles are ones in which the client sees the lawyer as an expert and the client in some respect as a novice. Cross-cultural clients can properly assume and accept that lawyers have substantial case-critical knowledge, skill, and experience that the client does not possess. The expert model for professional relationship may impact the form and detail of the lawyer's advice. Cross-cultural clients may desire to rely on the lawyer's expertise and judgment more than other clients, and on the lawyer's information less. Be sensitive to the client's preferences. Do not assume that the client always has an interest in hearing explanations or that the client wishes to reflect on detailed information about the law or strategy. Some cross-cultural clients are looking for straightforward answers from a lawyer who is willing to exercise the lawyer's expertise, rather than complex legal advice. Clients have the responsibility to make decisions about their matters. Yet they decide on a variety of levels of information and advice. Lawyers can adjust to clients' preferences so as not to unduly burden clients who prefer substantial expert support. Consider an example.

The more the lawyer attempted to explain the law through the translator, the more the client looked confused and uncertain. The translator seemed to struggle with the client's dialect as much as the client struggled with the translator's use of legal terms. Realizing the confusion, the lawyer began again, "You have done everything right." The client looked back now at the lawyer instead of looking uncertainly at the floor or wall. The lawyer continued, "Take these papers with you to the office." No more counseling, the lawyer decided. The lawyer's statements were now short, declarative, and authoritative.

"These papers?" the client asked through the translator. The lawyer took the papers again from the client's hands, reviewed them again briefly although this time silently rather than trying to explain them. The lawyer then reordered the papers to put a specific page on top and clipped them together again.

"Yes," the lawyer answered confidently, "They have them filled out right, and I have put them in the right order now." The client relaxed a little bit. "You have good people helping you," the lawyer said, adding, "They are some of the best in town. I have done this work before with them and seen it come out just right. You should trust them."

Finally, the client seemed relaxed and satisfied. The lawyer had not told the client why the papers were right or why she should trust the officials to whom the client was to return with the papers that the lawyer had just reviewed. Those explanations had only confused the client. The client needed no explanations from the lawyer, only that the lawyer would exercise his expertise on her behalf. The client gathered her papers, smiled at the lawyer in thanks, and left.

Non-Expert

On the other hand, other cross-cultural clients may be less willing to treat lawyers as experts and more interested in treating lawyers as non-expert providers of means and information. These clients may feel that they simply need the lawyer's information and access to forms and other resources—not the lawyer's recommendation, counseling, and advice. Clients of all socioeconomic classes and cultures can have substantial knowledge and expertise. Even when they do not have substantial knowledge and expertise, they may be unwilling to cede control over their matter to another, even to a professional like a lawyer. They may find more value in developing and exercising their own expertise than in relying on the expertise of lawyers and others.

Lawyers should be sensitive to cross-cultural clients' actual and asserted levels of expertise. Do not assume on the basis of bias or stereotype that the client needs or desires recommendations as to preferred options when to the contrary the client is prepared to decide and capable of deciding with only the lawyer's information. Clients make decisions on the goals and objectives of representation, not lawyers. Clients may also choose the means to achieve objectives. Lawyers can adjust to client preferences and respect client expertise and autonomy. Talking down to a cross-cultural client is unacceptable, particularly when the client has indicated the desire to exercise the client's own expertise or to develop that expertise. Consider an example.

"That's not what the website said," the scruffy homeless client shot back to the lawyer. The lawyer started to correct the client but then considered the resourcefulness that the client had already demonstrated in taking on the legal matter. The lawyer did not yet know the client's history as an advocate or his higher education level but could sense the client's interest in exercising or developing his own expertise.

"What did the website say?" the lawyer asked politely, ignoring the client's blunt and challenging manner. The lawyer could easily have explained the information that the client required but instead discerned that he should give the client a chance to demonstrate the client's own knowledge.

"The website said that there was another form," the client answered pulling another paper from his sack. The client handed it to the lawyer who laid it on the table between them right-side up to the client, upside-down to the lawyer. The lawyer already knew that the client had the wrong form but knew now that he should instead defer as much as possible to the client. The client was showing remarkable resourcefulness that the lawyer knew the lawyer should support.

"I can see you started to fill it out," the lawyer continued adding, "What made you stop?" The client smiled at the lawyer for the first time. Lawyer and client knew right then that they had settled on the right terms for the professional relationship. They would respect the expertise of one another.

"This question right here," the client pointed. The lawyer read the question aloud, upside down, and then stopped, waiting for the client. The client just looked back at the lawyer, this time waiting for the lawyer to acknowledge the client's actions.

"Yes, that's right, isn't it?" the lawyer smiled when he had finished reading, "This form doesn't apply, does it?" The client smiled back, shaking his head in agreement with the lawyer's judgment. The lawyer had passed the client's respect test, and so had the client passed the lawyer's. Lawyer and client saw one another on several occasions over the next two years. Each time, the client was significantly further along with his complex matter. Each time, the lawyer did little more in the consultation than confirm for the client that the client was heading in the right direction. The lawyer could have finished the whole matter for the client in short order but knew that the client was gaining much more by developing and exercising the client's own expertise.

"Even if current social theories favor classroom racial engineering as necessary to 'solve the problems at hand,' the Constitution enshrines principles independent of social theories. Indeed, if our history has taught us anything, it has taught us to beware of elites bearing racial theories. See *Dred Scott v. Sandford (1857)* ('They [members of the "negro African race"] had no rights which the white man was bound to respect'). Can we really be sure that the racial theories that motivated Dred Scott and Plessy are a relic of the past or that future theories will be nothing but beneficent and progressive? That is a gamble I am unwilling to take, and it is one the Constitution does not allow." Justice Clarence Thomas in *Parents Involved in Community Schools v. Seattle School Dist. No. 1,* 551 U.S. 701, 780-781 (2007), as quoted in JONATHAN BEAN, ED., RACE AND LIBERTY IN AMERICA: THE ESSENTIAL READER 40-41 (Univ. of Kentucky Press 2009).

Collective

Lawyers in their usual practices serving clients who embrace popular culture likely find those clients to be relatively individualistic in their thinking. Professional culture also tends toward individualism. When lawyer and client relate in the usual practice, they tend to relate as two individuals each with their own interests, even while recognizing that they each operate within constellations of others' interests. Cross-cultural clients may by contrast think and relate more in collective interest than individually. They may conceive of their legal matter less as an individual problem for them to resolve in their individual interest than as a need to determine and invoke a collective or common interest of the community of which they are a member.

The cross-cultural client who thinks and relates collectively may do so assuming that the lawyer is also a part of the client's group. The client may not conceive of the client's matter as distinct from the lawyer's personal interests and other professional matters but instead as the lawyer's equal responsibility as a part of the collective group. The client's inquiry would be less "What am *I* to do with *my* matter?" than "What are *we* to do with *our* matter?" or even "How will the community of which I am a part set this matter straight for itself?"

Cross-cultural clients may be more likely than other clients to treat the lawyer as an interdependent part of a communal self. Distinguish this horizontal collectivism in which all members of the group including the lawyer and client share in the responsibility for and control over each matter, with the vertical collectivism mentioned above in which clients can invoke the responsibility of lawyers and judges to act with authority over the clients' matters.

Collective thinking and relating is so unfamiliar to the popular and professional mind that it may seem to some lawyers as unwise, irresponsible, or immature. Yet horizontal collectivism can be a sound way of seeing relationships in many communities and circumstances. We are, in some circumstances, our brothers and sisters' keepers, especially when we have the expertise to help and when we stand in a professional relationship to another member of our community. Recognize the privilege of a cross-

187

cultural client seeing you as a part of the client's community, even as you recognize your additional responsibility under that form of lawyer-client relationship.

Resist the temptation to see collective-relating clients as shirking individual responsibility, especially when the client is indeed a part of a close and sharing community. Collective-relating clients may insist on disclosing the social or familial context to their legal matter even when not apparently relevant to the lawyer's advice. To the client, that information may not be irrelevant background but rather the client's description of the community interest that the client expects the lawyer to serve. The client may also invite the lawyer to make equivalent disclosures of the lawyer's social, familial, or other community context and interest. Collective-relating clients tend to see behavior as determined by social roles. Consider an example.

The cross-cultural client greeted the lawyer in the tiny conference room of the hive-busy church office of her close-knit congregation. The lawyer had taken years to learn the many family relationships spanning generations among the church members. Everyone was related to everyone else by blood, marriage, or children in common, it seemed. Weddings and funerals were huge affairs in which every member attended and many actively participated, some in multiple roles, planning, choreographing, speaking, dancing, cooking, and serving.

Lawyer and client first chatted amicably about family and church events of the past few weeks. The client graciously considered the lawyer a part of her church community, even though the lawyer was of a different ethnicity, education, vocation, and socioeconomic status—an outsider in so many respects but nonetheless committed to the welfare of this client and other community members. The lawyer listened to the client's conversation, trying to discern where the legal issue would arise. Eventually, the client's conversation turned to an overdue obligation that her adult son owed for which she was allegedly a co-signer. She opened her purse and pulled out the creditor's latest demand letter.

The lawyer sensed in the client's story that she may not have been a co-signer for her son's obligation. The client had implied as much, saying things like, "They think I owe this debt," without directly denying that she had helped her son open the account on which the son now owed the overdue obligation. The lawyer pressed the client only a little bit on whether she had co-signed. He understood her reluctance to call her son a forger on the account, although the conversation soon became clear to the lawyer that he probably was—that he had certainly opened the account by signing his mother's name to it when she had no intent that he do so.

The lawyer explained gently, almost circumspectly, that the mother could submit an affidavit of forgery and deny responsibility. He knew that the client would decline, which indeed she did. In a different client's community and vernacular, the son might have been a forger and deadbeat, and the mother an unwitting and unwilling facilitator of an irresponsible son. In this community, though, the lawyer knew the son to be selflessly devoted to the welfare of his mother and every other community member. Indeed, the lawyer knew no one else who was so selfless and without guile as was this client's son.

"How much can you and your son afford to pay?" the lawyer asked the client. The client explained the hardship that had led the son to default in the obligation. Lawyer and client discussed reasonable terms. The lawyer made a telephone call to the creditor and, over the next couple of weeks, worked out acceptable terms. The creditor, the lawyer knew, depended for his business on the trust of the same community. Even the creditor recognized that they were all in it together, looking out for one another.

> "Black people come from a collectivist culture because of our African ancestry that was traditionally rooted in a more collectivist culture or what is sometimes referred to as 'relational' or 'indigenous culture.' Most people of color come from these types of cultures. This was never clearer to me than when I had a very difficult conversation with an attorney who had just become the first black partner in his large law firm. I had been working with the firm on improving its diversity. I was thrilled for him, because he was an amazing

person and excellent lawyer. One day, soon after the announcement, I saw him and I excitedly congratulated him and commented about how proud he must be. I was not prepared for his response. He said, 'What do I have to be happy about? How can I be proud when there is no one here with me?' He went on to explain, that he would only be satisfied when he saw many more people of color coming up behind him. As long as his group still seemed to be having problems being hired and retained (there were very few attorneys of color in the firm), there was nothing to celebrate." Verna Myers, *Moving Diversity Forward—How to Go from Well-Meaning to Well-Doing* 85 (ABA 2011).

Reflections

Consider the following reflections on the above framework for recognizing and respecting a cross-cultural client's relationship practices and preferences. Add these reflections to your journal. Find an acquaintance with whom to discuss these questions, or organize a group discussion, to broaden and enrich your view:

1. Identify, if you are able, a different family member, friend, or acquaintance with whom you maintain each of the following relationships: (a) transactional; (b) relational; (c) expert; (d) non-expert; and (e) collective. Do your relationship forms differ from person to person? If so, then why?

2. Identify which of the following professional-relationship models you expect or prefer to follow with clients: (a) transactional; (b) relational; (c) expert; (d) non-expert; and (e) collective. Can you articulate why you have that preference?

3. For each of the following professional-relationship models, identify something that the client might say or do that would indicate to you that the client preferred that model: (a) transactional; (b) relational; (c) expert; (d) non-expert; and (e) collective.

4. For each of the following professional-relationship models, identify something that a client who preferred that form of professional relationship would *not* say or do: (a)

transactional; (b) relational; (c) expert; (d) non-expert; and (e) collective.

6. Identify one strength and one weakness of each of the following professional-relationship models: (a) transactional; (b) relational; (c) expert; (d) non-expert; and (e) collective. How, in each of those relationships, could you best draw on the strength and remediate the weakness?

7. For each of the following professional-relationship models, identify problems that may arise between you and the client if you have chosen the wrong model: (a) transactional; (b) relational; (c) expert; (d) non-expert; and (e) collective.

Chapter 12

Metacultural

"Can you help me, please?"

Immersion

The lawyer did not want to conduct the session, although he suspected that he would have to do so. The cultural center's executive director had given him just 48 hours of notice that as many as 100 of her constituents would be attending a question-and-answer session on workplace raids and deportation. "Can you help or find someone who can?" she asked.

The lawyer understood the need for the session. Immigration officials had recently conducted a major raid at a large local workplace. Fear, anger, and confusion rippled through the Hispanic-Latino community. The lawyer also understood why the executive director had asked him for help. He provided pro bono service at the center. The center's Hispanic-Latino staff and many of its patrons knew him and presumably trusted him. Yet giving general legal advice through a translator to a single non-English-speaking client at a time in the center's conference room was one thing. Presenting to a large upstairs roomful of individuals on a specialty subject—a controversial and difficult one at that, about which the lawyer knew little—was quite another. The lawyer wanted someone else to conduct the session, someone who knew more about immigration law and who could speak Spanish.

The lawyer made several emails and telephone calls with no success. Every immigration lawyer he asked had a schedule conflict, declined for fear of conflicts, or failed to get back to him. A couple of the lawyers gave him some reliable sources and tips. He did the research, developed a set of instructions, and headed for the center at the designated time just after work.

Spanish-speaking men and women filled the center's upstairs room, many of them with young children. Children ran back and forth playing games. The center's staff members were each busily registering attendees. The lawyer found it hard to find a place even to stand, no less to sit comfortably and reflect in preparation. He caught the executive director's eye across the room just to be sure that she knew he was present. She nodded a greeting but returned to intense conversation with several patrons.

As uncomfortable and out of place as he was, the lawyer was at the same time observing and adjusting. He nodded back and smiled at familiar and unfamiliar patrons. He would shrug and smile when a few tried asking him questions in Spanish. The lawyer noticed that it was more of a working crowd than he usually saw in his afternoon pro bono sessions. Families were also more evident. He also noticed fear and confusion mixed with the excitement of a relatively large gathering within this close-knit community.

The executive director called the session to order—in Spanish. The lawyer watched her demeanor closely and listened to the tone and pace of her voice. She spoke much more seriously and slowly than usual. Her statements were short, firm, and declarative. Her brow was knit with concern and her eyes filled with compassion, while her hands made broad gestures of confidence and reassurance. Then, she turned to the lawyer and nodded.

Mimicking the executive director's measured pace, serious tone, and compassionate demeanor, the lawyer began with a simple statement of deep concern, almost of apology. He let the love and emotion that he was right then feeling for these people to moisten his eyes, something that he never would have done in court or other professional settings. The lawyer then began with his series of simple statements of rights. Avoiding the use of legal terms, the lawyer said what individuals must do, need not do, and must not do when responding to enforcement measures. The executive director translated each of the lawyer's statements. The two of them took hardly a minute to adjust to one another. They were quickly speaking as one unified voice of concern and authority. As he had arranged with the executive director, the lawyer ended with an offer of the center's service for limited powers of attorney for guardianship of a minor.

Questions followed. The questions showed the lawyer that the patrons had understood and appreciated much of the direct advice. The lawyer's answers confirmed their understanding. The tone of the room had changed. Fear and confusion had turned once again to the resolve that had already carried the center's patrons farther than the lawyer could imagine his own resolve every carrying him. The event seemed to go about as well as possible. The executive director and staff seemed genuinely appreciative even if too busy once again with forms, questions, and embraces to do more than quickly thank the lawyer, who slipped out of the room and into the night for the long drive home.

Objectives

The first chapter ended with a statement of the book's objectives. For each of the five measures treated in the prior five chapters, (1) communication, (2) cognition, (3) resource, (4) reference, and (5) relationship, if you reflected productively on each chapter, then you should now be able to do each of the following activities in each of the five areas:

- identify your own practice;

- identify variety in client practices;

- distinguish your practice from your client's practice; and

- adjust your practice accordingly for effective advice and counsel to diverse clients.

Taken together, these objectives have a value well beyond their individual attainment. You should have noticed that each of the chapters on each of the above five measures gave five or so different models for that measure. Five models of five measures produces 5^5 (five to the fifth power) different possible individual profiles. Five to the fifth power equals 3,125 individual profiles. Think for a moment of the Myers Briggs Type Indicator assessment. That well-known personality-type assessment offers four measures, each of which has two alternatives: (1) extraversion or introversion; (2) sensing or intuition; (3) thinking or feeling; and (4) judgment or perception. The Myers Briggs test thus produces 2^4 or 16 different personality profiles. This book's model for idiographic assessment offers 3,125 different possible client profiles. Certainly, other measures and profiles exist. Yet within the five models of five measures you have a rich range for recognizing the diverse character, attributes, and preferences of cross-cultural clients, probably far more than you need, but still enough to give you a framework within which to develop sensitive skill.

Clients bring that variety. The individual clients mentioned in the illustrations above were from Sicily, Venezuela, Guatemala, Mexico, Colombia, Trinidad, Senegal, Nigeria, and other countries and regions around the world. They were African Americans, Hispanic-Latino Americans, European Americans, and Asian Americans. Some had graduate degrees. Others never finished middle school. The vignettes of them might not have shown it adequately, but they consistently graced the lawyer with whom they met. They spoke with smiles, hugs, high-fives, jokes, and secrets. On occasion, they shared candy bars, cookies, and thank-you notes, but most frequently and importantly trust and confidence. They laughed and cried, struggled and rejoiced, and most of all persevered. In each of them, the lawyer found something different, just as each of them found something different in the lawyer.

"The Task Force is aware that it answers its mandate and completes its work at a time of great national sensitivity to racial/ethnic and gender issues. We are confident that there is nothing in the accomplishment of our mandate that infringes upon the rights of any individual or any group; asks for unequal and preferential treatment for unqualified persons; or places an unfair burden upon organizations within our profession. To the contrary, the reporting of the status of the 1989 Supreme Court Task Forces' recommendations, and our recommendations for further implementation, go a long way toward increasing the quality of justice and credibility of the Michigan judicial system.

"The appearance of bias, as well as the reality of bias, damages our profession and our courts in their fundamental role as protector of freedom and dispenser of justice. In a very real sense, the implementation of these recommendations continues the process of insuring that the Michigan justice system accurately reflects the diversity of the constituency it serves, and that participants at all levels are afforded a level playing field upon which to operate. As we continue to strive for a bias-free society and justice system, lawyers, judges and their leaders must be in the forefront of this effort. This report, coupled with the 1989 Reports, will provide the members of our justice system with the knowledge and awareness needed to more ably continue this elusive undertaking." Executive Summary at 9, *Report of Task Force on Racial/Ethnic and Gender Issues in the Courts and Legal Profession* (State Bar of Michigan Jan. 23, 1998).

Meta-Cultural

The point of a lawyer's service, though, is not simply to find something different in clients but to *help them* with their legal matters. The idiographic model that this book offers actually has uses beyond supporting cross-cultural interaction. *Cross-cultural* implies interaction between a lawyer of one culture and a client of another. Lawyers can benefit by having cross-cultural skills, reaching out of their own professional culture to support a client who speaks, thinks, lives, and relates within another culture. Two of different cultures can interact from within their own culture when sensitive to the cultural differences of the other. So far, so good, right?

Yet again, the idiographic model that this book promotes has further purposes. *Intercultural* implies that lawyer and client may each adopt aspects of the other's culture. Lawyers can benefit by having inter-cultural skills, in which they are able not only to *recognize* but also to a certain extent *adopt* a client's cultural forms of speaking, thinking, living, and relating. A particularly effective lawyer may even become so skilled as not only to *modify* culture for its greatest effect in client service but even to *create* culture while also helping the client do so.

Ultimately, lawyers can exercise *meta-cultural* skill, using their trained powers of observing culture to discern, evaluate, and affect culture for its greatest client benefit. Meta-cultural skill begins with being cognizant of the effect of culture on one's self and others. Meta-cultural skill then extends to being able to modify thought and interaction to account for culture in a manner that maximizes human flourishing. Meta-cultural skill *transcends* culture. An effective meta-cultural lawyer can draw on and celebrate traditional culture while helping the client build new habits, practices, disciplines, and traditions. Culture does not determine human identity and destiny except to the extent that it remains unrevealed. Meta-cultural skill is simply *wisdom*, meaning the ability to apply the knowledge of situation and self to free one's self and others from that which destroys in favor of pursuing better relationships and life.

> "[P]resent in the story of Bethlehem and Jerusalem ... is a philosophy larger than other philosophies; larger than that of Lucretius and infinitely larger than that of Herbert Spencer. It looks at the world through a hundred windows where the ancient stoic or the modern agnostic only looks through one. It sees life with thousands of eyes belonging to thousands of different sorts of people, where the other is only the individual standpoint of a stoic or an agnostic. It has something for all moods of man, it finds work for all kinds of men, it understands secrets of psychology, it is aware of depths of evil, it is able to distinguish between real and unreal marvels and miraculous exceptions, it trains itself in tact about hard cases, all with a multiplicity and subtlety and imagination about the varieties of life which is far beyond the bald or breezy platitudes of most ancient or modern moral philosophy. In a word, there is more in it; it finds more in existence to think about; it gets more out of life. ... While it is deliberately broadened to embrace every aspect of truth, it is still stiffly embattled against every mode of error. It gets every kind of man to fight for it, it gets every kind of weapon to fight with, it widens its knowledge of the things that are fought for and against with every art of curiosity or sympathy; but it never forgets that it is fighting." G.K. CHESTERTON, THE EVERLASTING MAN (reprint Ignatius Press 1993 (Dodd, Mead & Co. 1925)).

A Professional Model

Wisdom calls the humble professional to a moral miracle-life of intensely pure and servant-like relations recognizing the unique, infinite, and inherent value and dignity of each client. All fields invite intercultural competence. The professional who fails to recognize and develop meta-cultural skills loses an opportunity and fails in an obligation to serve diverse clients. A meta-cultural professional identity includes an integrated and holistic worldview, one that makes sense of the world for the lawyer who holds that view. A meta-cultural identity includes some dimension of spirituality. It values relationship while supporting an intrinsic sense of self-worth. Its logic unifies and inquires rather than parses and divides. Meta-cultural skill enables a lawyer to assemble stories that symbolize profound truths.

Meta-cultural professional identity is not fragmented, materialistic, acquisitive, or overly individualistic. It does not assign value to clients based on achievement or other external characteristics. It is less deductive and does less counting and measuring. A meta-cultural lawyer is sensitive to diverse needs and knows diverse resources. A meta-cultural lawyer practices a theory of cross-cultural service that avoids inappropriate pathological attributions. A meta-cultural lawyer integrates the lawyer's own cultural and personal identity into professional settings. Meta-cultural competence combines satisfying exploration of self-knowledge with equally satisfying acquisition of concrete skills.

As suggested throughout above, the first step indeed must be in self-awareness—in developing cultural awareness. The exercises above have encouraged you to write your own narrative because it is in first understanding yourself that you begin to understand others better. Write your own narrative first before attempting to appreciate the narrative of others. An excellent way to learn about oneself is to see one's self in the character and challenges of others. We are all multicultural. Professional skill in serving diverse clients begins with recognizing one's own multicultural nature.

Reflections

Consider the following overall reflections on developing the professional skills and identity to serve diverse clients. Add these reflections to your journal. Find an acquaintance with whom to discuss these questions, or organize a group discussion, to broaden and enrich your view:

1. What is your personal ethnography? That is, describe the culture of which you are a part. Include appropriate references to your (a) country of origin, (b) ethnicity, (c) ancestry, (d) family of origin, (e) marital or present family, (f) socioeconomic status, (g) education, and (h) profession.

2. From your childhood or upbringing, identify three cultural markers, meaning three incidents, circumstances, or events that you now discern helped to shape your cultural identity or viewpoint.

3. From your professional education or practice, identify three additional cultural markers, meaning three incidents, circumstances, or events that you now discern helped to shape your cultural identity or viewpoint.

4. Use the five-dimension framework (communication, cognition, reference, resource, and relationship) to describe your overall habits and practices in interactions with clients or others around legal issues. What would clients say about you to others to describe how they would encounter you as a lawyer?

5. Identify three professional activities that you could undertake that would increase your interaction with unlike others in a way that could improve your cross-cultural skills. What are the first steps you would undertake to engage in each of those three activities? Whom would you contact? What time would you expect each activity to take?

6. Where are your community's greatest unmet needs in providing legal services to diverse clients? How could you contribute to meeting those needs?

7. How could your cross-cultural interests, activities, and commitments improve your work as a lawyer? What new resources might you acquire to serve your current clients? How could your new cross-cultural work improve your firm's bottom line? What additional client populations might you end up serving? What new law fields might you learn?

8. What summary statement would you like the local legal news to write regarding your outreach to unlike others when it gives notice of your retirement from law practice?

Bibliography

American Bar Association, *Building Community Trust: Improving Cross-cultural Communication in the Criminal Justice System* (June 2010).

Arredondo, Patricia, and Jeannette Gordon Reinoso, *Multicultural Competencies in Consultation*, in HANDBOOK OF MULTICULTURAL COMPETENCIES IN COUNSELING AND PSYCHOLOGY 330 (Sage Pub. 2003).

BALL, ARNETHA F., MULTICULTURAL STRATEGIES FOR EDUCATION AND SOCIAL CHANGE: CARRIERS OF THE TORCH IN THE UNITED STATES AND SOUTH AFRICA (Teachers College Press 2006).

Barkai, John, *What's a Cross-Cultural Mediator to Do? A Low-Context Solution for a High-Context Problem*, 10 CARDOZO J. CONFLICT RES. 43 (2008).

BEAN, JONATHAN, ED., RACE & LIBERTY IN AMERICA — THE ESSENTIAL READER (University of Kentucky Press 2009/The Independent Institute 2011).

Benchmark for Core Skills (First Draft), Palomar College (2007).

Brodie, Juliet M., *Post-Welfare Lawyering: Clinical Legal Education and a New Poverty Law Agenda*, 20 WASH. U. J.L. & POLY. 201 (2006).

Burton, Angela Olivia, *Cultivating Ethical, Socially Responsible Lawyer Judgment: Introducing the Multiple Lawyering Intelligences Paradigm into the Clinical Setting*, 11 CLINICAL L. REV. 15 (2004).

203

Bryant, Susan, *The Five Habits: Building Cross-Cultural Competence in Lawyers*, 8 CLIN. L. REV. 33 (2001).

Coleman, Hardin L.K., and Donald B. Pope-Davis, *Integrating Multicultural Counseling Theory*, in DONALD R. POPE-DAVIS AND HARDIN L.K. COLEMAN, EDS., THE INTERSECTION OF RACE, CLASS, AND GENDER IN MULTICULTURAL COUNSELING ix (Sage Pubs. 2001).

Constantine, Madonna G., and Derald Wing Sue, *The American Psychological Association's Guidelines on Multicultural Education, Training, Research, Practice, and Organizational Psychology: Initial Development and Summary*, in MADONNA G. CONSTANTINE AND DERALD WING SUE, STRATEGIES FOR BUILDING MULTICULTURAL COMPETENCE IN MENTAL HEALTH AND EDUCATIONAL SETTINGS 3 (John Wiley & Sons 2005).

D'Andrea, Michael, and Judy Daniels, *Respectful Counseling: An Integrative Multidimensional Model for Counselors*, in DONALD R. POPE-DAVIS AND HARDIN L.K. COLEMAN, EDS., THE INTERSECTION OF RACE, CLASS, AND GENDER IN MULTICULTURAL COUNSELING 417 (Sage Pubs. 2001).

Delgado-Romero, Edward A., Jessica Barfield, Benetta Fairley, and Rebecca S. Martinez, *Using the Multicultural Guidelines in Individual and Group Counseling Situations*, in MADONNA G. CONSTANTINE AND DERALD WING SUE, STRATEGIES FOR BUILDING MULTICULTURAL COMPETENCE IN MENTAL HEALTH AND EDUCATIONAL SETTINGS 39 (John Wiley & Sons 2005).

GANNON, MARTIN J., CULTURAL METAPHORS: READINGS, RESEARCH TRANSLATIONS, AND COMMENTARY (Sage Pubs. 2000).

Gloria, Alberta M., *The Cultural Construction of Latinas*, in DONALD R. POPE-DAVIS AND HARDIN L.K. COLEMAN, EDS., THE INTERSECTION OF RACE, CLASS, AND GENDER IN MULTICULTURAL COUNSELING 3 (Sage Pubs. 2001).

Hall, Gordon C.N., Irene R. Lopez, and Anita Bansal, *Academic Acculturation: Race, Gender, and Class Issues*, in DONALD R. POPE-DAVIS AND HARDIN L.K. COLEMAN, EDS., THE INTERSECTION OF RACE, CLASS, AND GENDER IN MULTICULTURAL COUNSELING 171 (Sage Pubs. 2001).

Hofstede, Geert, and Michael H. Bond, *The Confucius Connection: From Cultural Roots to Economic Growth*, in GANNON, MARTIN J., CULTURAL

METAPHORS: READINGS, RESEARCH TRANSLATIONS, AND COMMENTARY 31 (Sage Pubs. 2000).

Humber, Toni-Mokjaetji, *Intercultural Adaptations: A Stranger but Not Strange*, in MILLHOUSE, VIRGINIA H., MOLEFI K. ASANTE, AND PETER O. NWOSU, TRANSCULTURAL REALITIES: INTERDISCIPLINARY PERSPECTIVES ON CROSS-CULTURAL RELATIONS 227 (Sage Pubs. 2001).

Initial Interview Protocol, Thomas M. Cooley Law School Clinics (2007).

Jackson, Lisa R., *The Interaction of Race and Gender in African American Women's Experiences of Self and Other at a Predominantly White Women's College*, in DONALD R. POPE-DAVIS AND HARDIN L.K. COLEMAN, EDS., THE INTERSECTION OF RACE, CLASS, AND GENDER IN MULTICULTURAL COUNSELING 49 (Sage Pubs. 2001).

Kim, Min-Sun, *Perspectives on Human Communication: Implications for Transculture Theory*, in MILLHOUSE, VIRGINIA H., MOLEFI K. ASANTE, AND PETER O. NWOSU, TRANSCULTURAL REALITIES: INTERDISCIPLINARY PERSPECTIVES ON CROSS-CULTURAL RELATIONS 3 (Sage Pubs. 2001).

KUNDA, ZIVA, SOCIAL COGNITION: MAKING SENSE OF PEOPLE (MIT Press 1999).

Lakoff, George, and Mark Johnson, *Metaphors We Live By*, in GANNON, MARTIN J., CULTURAL METAPHORS: READINGS, RESEARCH TRANSLATIONS, AND COMMENTARY 3 (Sage Pubs. 2000).

LEBLANC, ADRIAN N., RANDOM FAMILY: LOVE, DRUGS, TROUBLE, AND COMING OF AGE IN THE BRONX (Scribner 2003).

Leong, Frederick T.L., and Aditya Bhagwat, *Challenges in "Unpacking" the Universal, Group, and Individual Dimensions of Cross-Cultural Counseling and Psychotherapy: Openness to Experience as a Critical Dimension*, in DONALD R. POPE-DAVIS AND HARDIN L.K. COLEMAN, EDS., THE INTERSECTION OF RACE, CLASS, AND GENDER IN MULTICULTURAL COUNSELING 241 (Sage Pubs. 2001).

Liu, William M., *Expanding Our Understanding of Multiculturalism: Developing a Social Class Worldview Model*, in DONALD R. POPE-DAVIS AND HARDIN L.K. COLEMAN, EDS., THE INTERSECTION OF RACE, CLASS, AND GENDER IN MULTICULTURAL COUNSELING 127 (Sage Pubs. 2001).

SHARAN B. MERRIAM & ANDRE P. GRACE, CONTEMPORARY ISSUES IN ADULT EDUCATION (John Wiley & Sons, Inc. 2011).

Mertz, Elizabeth, *Teaching Lawyers the Language of Law: Legal and Anthropological Translations*, 34 J. MARSHALL L. REV. 91 (2000).

MILLHOUSE, VIRGINIA H., MOLEFI K. ASANTE, AND PETER O. NWOSU, TRANSCULTURAL REALITIES: INTERDISCIPLINARY PERSPECTIVES ON CROSS-CULTURAL RELATIONS ix (Sage Pubs. 2001).

Mio, Jeffrey S., *On Teaching Multiculturalism: History, Models, and Content*, in GUILLERMO BERNAL, JOSEPH TRIMBLE, A. KATHLEEN BURLEW, AND FREDERICK LEONG, HANDBOOK OF RACIAL & ETHNIC MINORITY PYSCHOLOGY 119-120 (Sage Pub. 2003).

Mollen, Debra, Charles R. Ridley, and Carrie L. Hill, *Models of Multicultural Counseling Competence*, in HANDBOOK OF MULTICULTURAL COMPETENCIES IN COUNSELING AND PSYCHOLOGY 21 (Sage Pub. 2003).

MOODY, JOANN, FACULTY DIVERSITY—REMOVING THE BARRIERS (Routledge 2012).

Moore, Janet H., *The Culturally Savvy Associate: Top Three Tips for Moving Up in a Global Economy*, LAW PRACTICE (ABA 2010).

MOSKOVITZ, GORDON B., SOCIAL COGNITION: UNDERSTANDING SELF AND OTHERS (Guilford Press 2005).

Myers, Linda J., Ezemenari M. Obasi, Monica Jefferson, Michelle Anderson, Tamara Godfrey, and Jason Purnell, *Building Multicultural Competence Around Indigenous Healing Practices*, in MADONNA G. CONSTANTINE AND DERALD WING SUE, STRATEGIES FOR BUILDING MULTICULTURAL COMPETENCE IN MENTAL HEALTH AND EDUCATIONAL SETTINGS 109 (John Wiley & Sons 2005).

MYERS, VERNA, MOVING DIVERSITY FORWARD—HOW TO GO FROM WELL-MEANING TO WELL-DOING (ABA 2011).

NILE, LAUREN N., DEVELOPING DIVERSITY TRAINING FOR THE WORKPLACE: A GUIDE FOR TRAINERS 3-48 (NMCI Pubs. 9th ed. 2008).

Nussbaumer, John, *Misuse of the Law School Admissions Test, Racial Discrimination, and the De Facto Quota System for Restricting African-American Access to the Legal Profession,* 80 ST. JOHN'S L.REV. 167 (2006).

Ortony, Andrew, *Why Metaphors Are Necessary and Not Just Nice,* in GANNON, MARTIN J., CULTURAL METAPHORS: READINGS, RESEARCH TRANSLATIONS, AND COMMENTARY 9 (Sage Pubs. 2000).

Pedersen, Paul B., *Cross-Cultural Counseling: Developing Culture-Centered Interactions,* in GUILLERMO BERNAL, JOSEPH

Pedersen, Paul B., *Reducing Prejudice and Racism Through Counselor Training as a Primary Prevention Strategy,* in GUILLERMO BERNAL, JOSEPH TRIMBLE, A. KATHLEEN BURLEW, AND FREDERICK LEONG, HANDBOOK OF RACIAL & ETHNIC MINORITY PYSCHOLOGY 621 (Sage Pub. 2003).

Perez, Ruperto M., Mary A. Fukuyama, and Nancy C. Coleman, *Using the Multicultural Guidelines in College Counseling Centers,* in MADONNA G. CONSTANTINE AND DERALD WING SUE, STRATEGIES FOR BUILDING MULTICULTURAL COMPETENCE IN MENTAL HEALTH AND EDUCATIONAL SETTINGS 160 (John Wiley & Sons 2005).

Piomelli, Ascanio, *Cross-Cultural Lawyering by the Book: The Latest Clinical Texts and a Sketch of a Future Agenda,* 4 HASTINGS RACE & POVERTY L.J. 131 (2006).

Ponterotto, Joseph G., Jaclyn Mendelsohn, and Lonette Belizaire, *Assessing Teacher Multicultural Competence: Self-Report Instruments, Observer Report Evaluations, and a Portfolio Assessment,* in HANDBOOK OF MULTICULTURAL COMPETENCIES IN COUNSELING AND PSYCHOLOGY 191 (Sage Pub. 2003).

Quigley, Fran, *Seizing The Disorienting Moment: Adult Learning Theory and the Teaching of Social Justice in Law School Clinics,* 2 CLINICAL L. REV. 37 (1995).

ARIN N. REEVES, THE NEXT IQ: THE NEXT LEVEL OF INTELLIGENCE FOR 21ST CENTURY LEADERS (American Bar Association 2012).

Ridley, Charles R., Carrie L. Hill, Chalmer E. Thompson, and Alayne J. Ormerod, *Clinical Practice Guidelines in Assessment: Toward an Idiographic Perspective,* in DONALD R. POPE-DAVIS AND HARDIN L.K. COLEMAN, EDS.,

THE INTERSECTION OF RACE, CLASS, AND GENDER IN MULTICULTURAL COUNSELING 191 (Sage Pubs. 2001).

Sarat, Austin, "... *The Law Is All Over*": *Power, Resistance and the Legal Consciousness of the Welfare Poor*, 2 YALE J.L. & HUMAN. 343 (1990).

Thao, Mayia, & Mona Tawatao, *Developing Cultural Competence in Legal Services Practice*, CLEARINGHOUSE REV. J. POVERTY L. & POLICY 244 (September-October 2004).

TRIMBLE, A. KATHLEEN BURLEW, AND FREDERICK LEONG, HANDBOOK OF RACIAL & ETHNIC MINORITY PYSCHOLOGY 487 (Sage Pub. 2003).

Vasquez, Melba J.T., *Independent Practice Settings and the Multicultural Guidelines*, in MADONNA G. CONSTANTINE AND DERALD WING SUE, STRATEGIES FOR BUILDING MULTICULTURAL COMPETENCE IN MENTAL HEALTH AND EDUCATIONAL SETTINGS 91 (John Wiley & Sons 2005).

Wang, Vivian Ota, *Holding up Half the Sky: Reproductive Decision Making by Asian Women in America*, in DONALD R. POPE-DAVIS AND HARDIN L.K. COLEMAN, EDS., THE INTERSECTION OF RACE, CLASS, AND GENDER IN MULTICULTURAL COUNSELING 71 (Sage Pubs. 2001).

Weiss, Stephen E., *Negotiating with "Romans,"* in GANNON, MARTIN J., CULTURAL METAPHORS: READINGS, RESEARCH TRANSLATIONS, AND COMMENTARY 129 (Sage Pubs. 2000).

Wright, Walter A., *Practical Steps for Acquiring Cross-Cultural Negotiation Skills*, 70 TEX. B.J. 590 (July 2007).

LOIS J. ZACHARY, THE MENTOR'S GUIDE: FACILITATING EFFECTIVE LEARNING RELATIONSHIPS (Jossey Bass 2d ed. 2012).

Terminology

Acculturation: adaptations in practices, values, and beliefs one experiences when influenced by substantial contact with a culture unlike one's own.

Assimilation: adopting the practices, values, and beliefs of the dominant culture in which one operates.

Bias: making assumptions (positive or negative) about a client based on class, culture, or other presumed group characteristics. Compare to "prejudice."

Class: a grouping of clients traditionally by income level such as lower-income, middle-income, upper-income, etc., in order to infer statuses helpful to informed legal advice.

Cognition: the mental practices, processes, and habits a client uses in order to understand and act on a lawyer's information and advice.

Competence: a level of recognition-based skill that will adequately serve the needs of a client.

Cross-cultural: relating to interaction between two different sets of common practices, values, and beliefs of groups identifiable by race, class, locale, and other characteristic or attribute.

Cultural: based on or influenced by the common practices, values, and beliefs of a group that is identifiable by race, class, locale, and other characteristic or attribute.

Diverse: client characteristics, attributes, and practices that vary in a significant way likely to affect legal advice, from those which a lawyer usually experiences.

Enculturation: the unnoticed immersion of a lawyer into professional habits and practices that influence the lawyer's conduct toward clients.

Framework: an organized and well-thought-out conceptual structure a lawyer can use to inform and guide the lawyer's professional attitude and practices toward a client.

Idiographic: identifying and comprising the specific attributes of a person or situation distinct from presumption based on group associations and surrounding culture.

Meta-cultural: cognizant of the effect of culture on one's self and others, and able to modify thought and interaction to account for culture while maximizing human flourishing.

Misattribution: assigning the wrong goals, objectives, or intent to a client because of bias, prejudice, or misunderstanding.

Mono-cultural: representative of the common practices, values, and beliefs of a single group identifiable by race, class, locale, and other characteristic or attribute.

Multicultural: representative of the common practices, values, and beliefs of a variety of groups identifiable by race, class, locale, and other characteristic or attribute.

Nomothetic: a description derived from general observations of personality traits common to a group or culture.

Pathological: a quality of a behavior that undermines the person exhibiting it and persons with whom the exhibiter comes into contact or relationship.

Prejudice: holding negative feelings about a client based on class, culture, locale, and other presumed group characteristics, and expressing those negative feelings in treatment of the client.

Professional: based on or influenced by the approved practices of skilled and ethical lawyers.

References: the traditions, concepts, and meanings a client's communication, demeanor, dress, and other observable characteristics would suggest to a skilled and sensitive observer.

Register: language levels or patterns reflecting a client's habits of thinking. We recognize five language registers above.

Relationship: the inherent nature and essential quality of the ongoing interaction between lawyer and client.

Resource: the broad variety of available means (finances, contacts, skills, etc.) by which a client can further the client's own objectives.

Sensitive: observant, aware, and capable of making positive use of subtle features of a client's communication, goals, objectives, and intent.

Socioeconomic: related to the client's social environment and economic status such as majority homeless, minority low-income, immigrant middle-income, etc.

Stereotype: an incorrect image of a client constructed from prior experience with other clients assumed to be alike, and likely to adversely affect the legal advice and lawyer/client relationship.

Acknowledgments

Credit for supporting the research and drafting of this book goes to Western Michigan University Cooley Law School where the authors are professors and deans of its Grand Rapids campus. Credit also goes to the school's founder the Honorable Thomas Brennan for establishing the school's access mission and to the school's President and Dean Don LeDuc for supporting that access mission. Credit for some of the ideas, practices, tools, and sources in this book goes to the West Michigan College and University President's Diversity Compact, its member schools, and its staff leaders. The Compact has contributed significantly to diversity work on the law school's Grand Rapids campus.

The authors also credit the diversity-and-inclusion work of the Grand Rapids Bar Association and its member judges and lawyers and their firms, particularly Joy Fossel of Varnum, Stephen Drew of Drew Cooper Anding, Mary Bauman of Miller Johnson, Rodney Martin of Warner Norcross, Patrick Miles formerly of Dickinson Wright and now U.S. Attorney for the Western District of Michigan, the Honorable Benjamin Logan III, and Bar Association President Thomas Behm, Past Presidents Mark Smith, T.J. Ackert, and Kristin Vanden Berg, and Executive Director Kim Coleman.

While the writing in this book is original, the authors relied on previously published, coauthored works. The authors drew concepts from the article *The Role of Law Schools in Shaping Culturally Competent Lawyers*, 89/1 MICH. BAR J. 16 (2010), co-authored with Cooley Assistant Dean Cynthia Ward; *Cultural Competence as a Professional Skill* co-authored with Cooley Assistant Dean Tracey Brame, Professor Kim O'Leary, and Adjunct Professor Dale Iverson, in AMY TIMMER & NELSON MILLER, EDS., REFLECTIONS OF A LAWYER'S SOUL—THE INSTITUTIONAL EXPERIENCE OF PROFESSIONALISM AT THOMAS M. COOLEY LAW SCHOOL (William S. Hein & Co. 2008); and the article *Equality as Talisman: Getting Beyond Bias to Cultural Competence as a Professional Skill*, 25 COOLEY L. REV. 100 (2008), co-authored with WMU-Cooley Professor Kim O'Leary and Adjunct Professor Dale Iverson. These coauthors deserve rich credit for supporting those works, as do the publishers.

The authors drew other concepts from the article *Beyond Bias: Cultural Competence as a Lawyer Skill*, 87/6 MICHIGAN BAR JOURNAL 38 (2008); the book chapter *Instruction in Meta-Ethical Competence*, in AMY TIMMER & NELSON MILLER, EDS., REFLECTIONS OF A LAWYER'S SOUL—THE INSTITUTIONAL EXPERIENCE OF PROFESSIONALISM AT THOMAS M. COOLEY LAW SCHOOL (William S. Hein & Co. 2008); and the article *Meta-Ethical Competence as a Lawyer Skill: Variant Ethics Affecting Lawyer and Client Decision-Making*, 9 T.M. COOLEY J. PRACTICAL & CLIN. L. 91 (2007). These publishers deserve credit for supporting those works.

The authors particularly wish to acknowledge and thank Dr. Tim Ready, Director of Western Michigan University's Lewis Walker Race & Ethnic Relations Institute, for his manuscript comments. While the authors are solely responsible for this book's contents, the authors highly value Dr. Ready's insights, which helped them adjust and correct some of the manuscript's inevitable errors and distortions. We all see through our own lenses only darkly. The perspective of others, particularly those as wise as Dr. Ready, can help each of us see more truth and err less badly and less often.

About the Authors

Nelson Miller is professor and associate dean at Western Michigan University Thomas M. Cooley Law School. Before joining WMU-Cooley, Dean Miller practiced civil litigation for 16 years, representing individuals, corporations, agencies, and public and private universities. He has published 25 books and dozens of book chapters and articles on law and law practice. The State Bar of Michigan recognized Dean Miller with the John W. Cummiskey Award for pro-bono service. He earned his law degree at the University of Michigan while working for the law firm that later became Fajen and Miller, PLLC, where after nearly 30 years he remains of counsel. Dean Miller teaches courses in Torts, Civil Procedure, Professional Responsibility, Employment Law, and Interviewing and Counseling, among other subjects. Harvard University Press included Dean Miller among 26 law professors featured in its book *What the Best Law Teachers Do*.

Tracey Brame is professor and assistant dean at Western Michigan University Thomas M. Cooley Law School. Before joining WMU-Cooley, Dean Brame advised and represented low-income clients as a staff attorney for Legal Aid of Western Michigan, represented indigent clients as a staff attorney for Public Defender Services for the District of Columbia and an assistant defender with the State Appellate Defender Office in Detroit, and served as a research-and-writing specialist with the Federal Defender Office. Dean Brame also served as a law clerk to the Honorable Julian Abele Cook, Jr., of the U.S. District Court in Detroit, with the Federal Defender Office, and with Scott Correctional Facility, after earning her law degree at the

University of Michigan. She also advocated for clients of the Alabama Capital Resource Project and drafted racial-justice legislation for the Alabama. Dean Brame founded and currently co-directs the law school's Access to Justice Clinic and Public Defender Clinic at the Grand Rapids campus, while teaching courses in Family Law, Race and the Supreme Court, and Interviewing and Counseling, and a Death Penalty Seminar.

www.ingramcontent.com/pod-product-compliance
Lightning Source LLC
Chambersburg PA
CBHW072120020426

42334CB00018B/1664